the soul under siege

(A Fresh Look at Christian Experience)

james earl massey

*For Doctor Roy Blackwood:
with appreciation
and warm regards
James Earl Massey
phil. 1: 20-21*

**THE WARNER PRESS
ANDERSON, INDIANA**

B1025

To my parents
George and Elizabeth
who by precept and example
introduced me to the joys of
Christian living

Contents

Preface

This book takes a fresh look at Christian experience, using the seizure of the soul (in conviction, temptation, stress experiences) as the special point of focus. It is always in order to give a periodic restatement of Christian truths and trace out guidelines for persons serious about living the Christian life.

The title and subtitle were framed with deliberate intent, and the materials which fill the chapters have been shaped and tested by prolonged exposure to many other minds and lives. This book is a kind of excursion into the theology of Christian experience. The subject of Christian experience is vast. It involves issues and problems and concerns that call upon materials and insights from many fields—particularly biblical studies, theology, philosophy, ethics, and psychology.

The present study is admittedly limited in its scope and aim. So much has been left unsaid or left without the elaboration some readers would expect. The popular nature of the treatment meant that some omissions and curtailments would have to occur. Documentation has had to be restricted in the interests of popular style and brevity of space. The basic point of the book, cast in the form of theological musings, is to take a fresh look at the subject of Christian experience. The book celebrates the reality of new life in Christ for the man who follows him with earnest intent.

PREFACE

The basic substance of this book has been shared in both church and academic settings, worship occasions and campus gatherings. The campus community of Anderson College heard some of these themes during Religious Emphasis Week. The call to speak on that occasion permitted me to focus a longtime concern that was in keeping with the week itself.

President Robert H. Reardon was especially kind in his regard for the aptness of the presentations; and Dean Robert A. Nicholson, Professor Marie Strong, and Dean Gene W. Newberry of the Graduate School of Theology, enriched my stay with their characteristic courtesies.

The same must be said in tribute to President Frank B. Stanger, President-emeritus Julian C. McPheeters, Dean Turkington, and the Reverend Robert Fraley, during my appearance as speaker at Asbury Seminary, Wilmore, Kentucky. The student body gave attentive ear and evidenced in many other ways regard for the central thrust of these pages.

Portions of the material were also used in addressing several faculty and student groups in Jamaica, West Indies; Jamaica Theological Seminary and Mico College, both in Kingston; and Moneague Training College, located at Moneague, Jamaica. I also used some of this material while serving as speaker during Mission Week at The University College of the West Indies, at Mona Campus, Kingston.

Portions of this book have appeared in abridged form as articles in *Vital Christianity*. Appreciation is gratefully extended to Mrs. Mabel Wilson and Miss Mary Smith, office secretaries of Metropolitan Church, and Mrs. Evelyn B. Small, who was responsible for typing the final copy in its entirety.

1: The Christian Self

I sat one evening to watch a telecast version of Lewis Carroll's *Alice in Wonderland*. There was a scene during which Alice confronted a questioning caterpillar. The caterpillar looked Alice over with his experienced eyes, and then asked her this question, "Who are you?" The question was both fair and simple enough, but its importance was heightened when young Alice replied, "I—I hardly know, Sir." Alice then asked the questioning caterpillar who he was, but he bypassed the problem and never really answered. He shrewdly changed the subject.

Who are *you?* Life has made this question of identity both essential and commanding for us all. Just how do you see yourself? What about yourself has been obvious to your sight? What stands clearly marked off in your experience as *you?* Through what crises have you discovered more details about what *you* are?

These questions help us to recall how sensitive we have been during those revealing moments when life made us look seriously at ourselves. Let us look again, intent this time upon a spiritual mission in the behalf of *self.*

"Know thyself," the dictum runs. But full knowledge does not come easily. The very nature of our lives makes the task quite hard. Nevertheless, we cannot long shy away from the attempt to know ourselves because every crisis makes us candidates for self-discovery. The desire to know himself presses upon every man who has ever seriously faced himself.

The quest to know begins very early. I remember asking my niece Marcia that question ("Who are you?")

when she was two years old. I was holding her in my arms and had asked her to identify different objects around in the room. She did quite well. Helen, her mother, walked into the room. I pointed to Helen and asked, "Marcia, who is that?" She answered in two-year-old fashion, "Mommy!" Intent to test her *self*-awareness at that age, I placed my finger against Marcia's shoulder and asked, "And who is that?" She smiled, knowingly, and coyly replied, "Me." Marcia continues to this day to explore the fact of herself. And so do we all. No person lives without being concerned about the fact of himself. The quest to know ourselves begins even earlier than the tender age of two. It continues well beyond the full age of eighty-two. There is within us all a distinct sense of self and a lifelong desire to know that self to a satisfying and useful degree.

A report has it that a certain man walked along a street in Berlin one day, pacing back and forth undaunted by the falling rain. When he finally sat down on a nearby bench, an observing policeman approached and questioned him. The policeman addressed the shabbily dressed fellow with that question, "Who are you?" The man paused in his pondering and raised a sad face to the officer; his voice was filled with deep longing as he replied, "I wish that I knew. I do, indeed, wish that I knew." His name was Arthur Schopenhauer. But knowing his name did not grant that philosopher a sufficient knowledge about himself. Schopenhauer knew his name but did not understand his nature.

Every man has had to pace, pondering the question and seeking insight into himself. Man is a thinking creature who is pushed by crisis and by curious concern to examine his moorings in life and penetrate the questions raised by the fact of his human self. Self-knowledge does not come easily; nor does our rewarded scrutiny of self allow us to rest in ease once the multitudinous facts about ourselves begin to pile up before us.

Every man has had to face pondering the question and He knows that he holds within himself an investment that is of value beyond himself. This sense of value is not only a personal resource that causes a man to honor and regard himself. It also helps a man to understand and regard all other men. The man who properly values himself is also aware that a unity binds all humans into a special whole; he will therefore exercise a care and concern that will even make him exhaust himself in efforts to help another man in times of extreme need.

Dr. T. Franklin Miller tells of being on a ship at sea and having to miss his scheduled arrival time in Montreal because his ship went to the rescue of a man, deathly sick, on another ship about five hundred miles away. The ship on which Dr. Miller was sailing had a surgeon and hospital facilities, while the ship bearing the sick man did not have them. There was nervous excitement aboard the passenger liner as that ship hurried toward the stricken man. When the needed rendezvous was completed, the sick man was transferred by lifeboat to the passenger vessel, and surgery was performed on him with successful results. The passenger liner docked at its destination one day late, and nine hundred passengers were afflicted with complications with train, bus, and air travel connections: all because of *one man*—one man in need!

How did the passengers react to the change of plans? Dr. Miller talked with several of them during the time of travel to rescue the stricken man. The surprising observation was that not one person with whom he conversed had a single note of criticism about the rescue action. In spite of the personal inconveniences, everybody seemed pleased that their ship could assist a man in distress. That reaction was something other than a matter of just being nice about the inevitable delay. Every passenger was alert to the concern he felt for the man in need. Despite the altered course and the forced changes in personal plans, the one in need was *a man,* and aiding him was the most important matter to be handled at that time.

A human being is a figure of importance, a creature of mystery and inestimable worth. This is recognized even by those who do not operate from within the concerns of religious views. But those who are informed by religious concerns know that it takes God to fully assess a man. They also know that it takes God to fully explain him.

At our mention of the word "man" several traditions of thought stand mingled in our minds. One tradition is the Hebrew view of man, the view set forth in the early chapters of Genesis where Adam and Eve are the central human figures. A second tradition is from Greek thought, in which man is viewed as unique in the world because he is a reasoning creature with the capacity and concern to search his life and surroundings and frame a view of the nature of things. A third tradition about man is scientific and more recent: it is the product of special studies about the nature of human life, with views and findings supported by scientific inquiry. There are essential points of agreement among all three of these traditions. There are also significant points of difference between them, especially the question of the origin, purpose, and destiny of man.

THE CHRISTIAN SELF

Despite the apparent and real differences, however, there is a unique contribution that each tradition has made to our understanding of ourselves. The biblical view of man asserts and declares *from above,* as it were: it discloses the human position in relation to God who created and companions man. The philosophic and scientific views of man speak about him *from the side* or *from within;* these show us man alone or with his own kind, while the biblical view shows us the life of man in the light of God.

The Natural Self: (1) Insights from Science

The strong desire on the part of man to know himself has prompted questioning minds to develop studies about our lives and nature. A sustained attempt has been made to determine what is our measure as human beings. The studies continue to appear, and the theories about the human measure are multitudinous indeed. In a book published in 1937, author Gordon W. Allport cited as many as fifty different views advanced by psychologists about the human "personality." Each theorist had held man at close range for pointed study, questioning his nature, examining his actions, and venturing to suggest his possibilities. The examinations have continued, with clinic and classroom having joined hands in hope and interest. Vital considerations continue to be amassed about our kind through scientific effort. The various fields of science have helped us to develop new and needed understanding of ourselves; they have provided scientific detail to common sense data, illuminating facets of our lives with special intent. The literature is vast that deals with how we think, how we feel, how and why we act, the attitudes we hold, the powers we exercise, and our positioned life as dependent beings in a real, wide, ordered, natural world.

1. Scientific probing has exposed more facts about ourselves as *persons*. Our awareness about our conscious, individual lives has been sharpened. Scientific probing has helped us to delineate our personal uniqueness as separate selves. It has helped us to realize the intricate pattern of features that separate one man from another, those features that identify each of us as an individual person, "sole, unitary, unprecedented, and unrepeatable," as John Wright Buckham put it. It is largely with these dimensions of similarity and difference that the study of personality seeks to deal.

2. The scientific view of self has helped us to understand ourselves better as *products*. Many streams of influence flow into every man. The effects of that "in-flow" can be seen in our looks, our physical structure, our blood characteristics, our mental and physical health, and even the anticipated life-span. The body of every man is living, vivid evidence that he did not just "happen." Every one of us is a product, made and marked in our physical and mental design by several streams of influence.

3. The scientific picture of man has provided more detail about ourselves as *participants*. Every man is a dependent being; he stands related to a world of other persons and things. Scientific studies have advanced our cause by supplying needed knowledge about how to make the physical world around us sustain and further our lives. Those studies have guided us in mobilizing our capacities to achieve needed results in our common life together as social creatures. Both nature and other persons are neces-

sary to us; they are essential to an adequate and creative style of life. The bequeathments of science have helped us to properly combine our abilities and focus our intent as living sharers.

4. A great deal of scientific detail has also been offered about the fact that every man is *pliable*. We can and do undergo change.

We humans are impressionable. We can develop. We can adapt ourselves. We can learn. We can bring about radical innovations in our lives by means of thought, will, and sustained intent. Numerous studies tell of the combinations of experience possible for us as growing, changing persons. They help us to sharpen our awareness of what we experience. Those studies have illumined the intricacies of *personal* life; for instance, the reliable data on childhood, youth, adulthood, and aging have placed many materials for self-understanding at our disposal.

5. Despite the changes that we experience, however, there is within each of us a stable and identifiable life: the self is *perduring*. There is a central inward agency that is the custodian of all else that changes. It is the deepest and most mysterious part of ourselves. Some speak of it as the "soul." Some others refer to that custodian as the "ego." By whatever label, it is that part of the self that uniquely perdures, that hidden part of ourselves where life is focused and realized and regulated.

I remember a conversation with my oldest brother, George, after a visit he had made at the home of our parents. During his stay with them, George had spent some time perusing the family photograph album. As he leafed through the pictures, he had to stop now and again, he

15

said, to chuckle. The years had made such a noticeable difference in how we looked during childhood, when those pictures were made, and how we now look as adults. When he told me about his feelings when viewing those pictures we both laughed. I, too, had seen them. But there was something more basic that crept into my thinking: despite all the recognized change and growth, there was still the fact that the pictures were of us. Something deeper than the shape of our heads or the set of our young eyes was there. The very fact that we could *remember* those earlier years surely focused a *personal* understanding in our minds. Something in each of us had remained constant in the midst of the passing years. The literature of science is filled with studies that help to analyze the development of the self we remember and look back upon with such personal concern. Considerations of the self as a perduring agent form a large part of the scientific literature on the subject of personality.

6. Scientific studies have had to deal with another fact writ large in life concerning our kind: man is *perverted*. Something within man is distorted, something that blights the adventure of living and makes life an experience of frustrating anxiety. The knowledge that "something is not right within" affects the moods of the self, muddles the motives, and constantly reminds a man that he is not at his best. The problem is peculiar, pointed, personal, and persistent. Studies steadily appear dealing with this evident uneasiness; they are seeking to account for the deep discontent and discord within the self. The answers and proposed solutions to this problem do vary, but all the major thought about the human self has recognized that a basic perversion has blighted man.

THE CHRISTIAN SELF

The Natural Self: (2) Insights from Scripture

The Bible tells us that the ground of that human uneasiness is sin. Man has fallen into conflict with himself because he has fallen from the moral and spiritual level of life on which God willed that he live. This fall has brought him into conflict with God. The central message of the Bible is how that conflict can be remedied and a level of communion with God regained.

Man began life as a creation of God, uniquely formed "in the image of God" (Genesis 1:27). According to the Genesis story, the Lord God formed man of dust from the ground, and breathed into his nostrils the breath of life; "and man became a living being" (2:7). Standing alive "in the image of God," man began life as a unique self: he was rooted in a natural world but bore within himself something that made him stand uniquely above what is only natural.

The unity between man and the natural world is self-evident. There is no need to remark about it here. But that phrase "in the image of God" has never failed to raise questions. It has been especially important to exegetes, theologians, philosophers, and psychologists. The comments about its meaning have been quite varied, but all have basically agreed that "in the image of God" describes something special, something unique that made (and/or makes) man, *man*. Theologians seem agreed that the phrase means that man is like God in that he is rational and moral, free, self-transcending, with personal qualities that distinguish him from the animals. Man can think, communicate his thoughts, and even think about himself.

The *full* dimensions of this biblical phrase continue to elude us, but we can be certain that the phrase provides

us with a biblical measure for ourselves at our best—
"best" here meaning God's intention for us. The phrase
tells us God's assessment of man when he was first shaped
and stood alive. The phrase tells us that man possesses
something in measure that God possesses in fullness. It
keeps our view centered upon the fact that we can never
dispense with the pattern God willed for human life without disruption and distortion appearing in ourselves. The
phrase stays with us to speak remindingly about the di-
vine-human relationship. When that relationship was lost,
man became disrupted and distorted within himself. The
Bible uniquely locates the source of human perversion.
The Bible also tells of God's provided means for the
needed human change.

"So God created man . . . , " the Genesis account tells
us (1:27). According to the story there, everything issued
from the activity of God. The first man was conscious of
his origin. He was also conscious of his role under God.
This fact in the story is worthy of increased attention. But
before the arrival of man on the earth, God had created
and shaped the earth for habitation and development.
From the first, God is seen as altogether above nature:
he is responsible for nature, and he superintends it as the
sole, supreme, and active God. He is related to the whole
creation as creator and sustainer.

This subject was so important that the writer of this
account used the elevated style of the epic to express the
truth about God's creation of the world and its chief in-
habitant, man. The whole pattern of the writer's work
blends literal and figurative elements in order to teach
a theology. He was saying that the world in all its fullness
stands as a product of the God of the Hebrews. He was

declaring that the foundations of nature and human life are theological. This is a positive point in both Genesis and the rest of Scripture.

In depicting and discussing man, Scripture does not inquire, it sets forth; it declares. Scripture declares: man is a creature of God, made "in the image of God." Scripture declares: man is a part of the unity of nature, set in the natural order, but he has qualities and capacities which make him rise higher than mere nature; he is distinct and unique in creation. The descriptive language about the creation of man has its reason. In the shaping of man something happened without analogy in the rest of nature: a being was shaped "in the image of God." It is even proper to say that in the creation of man, "God participated more intimately and intensively than in the creation of his earlier works."

Man cannot be properly understood *in* and *by* himself. Humanity is not self-subsisting. We cannot be detached from life with God without extreme consequences to ourselves and to *all of nature*. The teaching of Genesis 3 seeks to make this point clear. The writer of Psalm 139 must have had the closeness of God and man in mind when he soliloquized about how his whole life was embedded in God's determinations for him, and how he was so utterly dependent upon God's dealings in his behalf:

For thou didst form my inward parts,
  thou didst knit me together in my mother's womb.
I praise thee, for thou art fearful and wonderful.
  Wonderful are thy works!
Thou knowest me right well;
  my frame was not hidden from thee,

THE SOUL UNDER SIEGE

when I was being made in secret,
  intricately wrought in the depths of the earth.
Thy eyes beheld my unformed substance;
  in thy book were written, every one of them,
the days that were formed for me,
  when as yet there was none of them. (vss. 13-16)

He rightly prayed to be searched and tried and led by God, lest some inward wickedness cause him to go astray from the God by whom he lived.

We cannot understand ourselves *in* and *by* ourselves. It takes the God who made us to explain us to ourselves. We do not know ourselves aright, apart from the illuminating word of Scripture. When we attempt to explain ourselves without recourse to God and his word, we fall into further distortion and disturbance. We can know ourselves in truth only as we see ourselves in the light of God. The proper study of mankind is therefore man before God and not man alone. The life of man is full only when he lives with God fully in his life. Linnaeus, the Swedish naturalist, was mindful of this as he read the searching lines of Psalm 139. He was so impressed by the psalmist's sense of God and his relationship to Him that he soon placed a reminding inscription over the door of his lecture room, *Innocui vivite, Numen adest*—"Live innocently, God is here." The failure of man has been to disregard the presence and will of his creator. Inward discord is his realized result.

The Christian Self

In one of his notebooks written while he was at Dresden, Arthur Schopenhauer wrote: "Inward discord is the very law of human nature, so long as a man lives. He can be only one thing actually and thoroughly; and yet for everything else he has a potentiality, and an inextirpable possibility of becoming it." He continued, "Now one, now another principle gains the upper hand, while he is the field on which the combat is fought. Even though the one be continually victorious, still the other is continually fighting; for as long as he lives, it lives. As a human being, he is the possibility of many contrasts. Such being the case, whence can inward harmony be found?" The New Testament deals with that question and need. It is filled with "notes" from the lives of men whose question had been answered and whose inner need had been handled. They all wrote about a saving encounter with Jesus the Christ. The theme of the New Testament is how a confused, corrupted self can become a corrected, converted, Christlike self. The message of its pages is that there is a way under God to find the needed "inward harmony."

The writings of Paul, in particular, give us a somewhat extensive exposition of this needed and possible change. Paul had also seen and known the basic antagonism that lies within a discordant and disrupted self. His picture of a broken self as recorded in Romans 7 is immediately recalled and is very familiar. That warring man in the chapter questioned his unsatisfactory state of mind and being. He lamented: "Wretched man that I am! Who will deliver me from this body of death?" (vs. 24). But he went on immediately to confess the way that relief and satisfaction came. He exclaimed, "Thanks be to God through Jesus Christ our Lord!" (vs. 25a). He had seen and known something about himself that made him lament his life and inward affairs. Now a change having been provided for him through Christ, the old lament has become past history because a new history of self has begun.

Ralph Waldo Emerson in his essay on "The Over-Soul" asked the same question as the man in Romans 7: "What is the ground of this uneasiness of ours, of this old discontent?" The New Testament supplies clear answers. It also states the supplied remedy to handle that uneasiness. The remedy is conversion, newness, change through encounter with Christ. Paul referred to this when he wrote: "Therefore, if anyone is in Christ, he is a new creation; the old has passed away, behold, the new has come" (2 Cor. 5:17). Paul write to celebrate and explain the fact of a new human condition. He was speaking from inside about the experience of being a Christian self. Nowhere does Paul reveal his concern more fully than in his treatment of this theme and its implications for the total self. But Paul was not alone in his concern; that concern was matched by the common experience of the other New Testament writers and an innumerable host of other believers.

The man who believes on Christ becomes immediate heir to a new condition and quality of life for which Christ is uniquely responsible. It is Christ who determines the change experienced by the believer. The believer is forever dependent upon Christ for the progressive stages of the new life. The New Testament is filled with basic texts and passages that outline, describe, and celebrate the reality of the Christian self.

The new life as a Christian self means a new experience that is initiated and indwelt by Christ. An "ex-

THE CHRISTIAN SELF

perience" involves a personal relationship to something or someone; and a man must be conscious of that relationship to some extent as his very own concern before it registers within him as *his* experience. As for Christian experience, this is what a man realizes when a correspondence has been established between himself and God in Christ. The correspondence begins when the old self stands confronted by the realized claims of God in Christ. The encounter is awesome. A radical claim is made upon the self to submit, to yield, to agree with the righteous demands of God.

The self feels strangely unstable because a divine center of authority confronts the self, challenging it to account for itself. The sense of the Holy exposes and searches the faultiness and sin of the old life. The result is the awesome feeling of *exposed individuality*—being before God, and being there in an unworthy state of soul. The encounter with God through his personal claims in Christ is actually realized as an experience, a personal experience of confrontation. The confrontation exacts some kind of response. If the response is proper, the self surrenders to the claims of Christ. A relationship results, together with the beginning of a conscious, substantive change in one's personal style of life. The character is affected. Dimensions of meaning are sensed upon which reflection will have to be done and categorizing take place.

Christian experience is always the work of Christ in response to a surrendered self. Something is always deposited in the life, something that can be regarded, remembered, reflected upon, and developed. Christian experience is historical, derivative, personal, supernatural in origin.

THE SOUL UNDER SIEGE

It is the result of identification with Christ and participation in his chosenness, his character, and even his commitment. It involves the whole man and his whole life. To say that one is a Christian is to say that the whole range of his human experience has been brought under the influence and presence of the person of Christ. Such a man will spend the rest of his life realizing what was initiated by the encounter and surrendering further to the call of Christ to follow him.

The Christian self is a changed self, a converted self. The change is both real and radical. The self is not merely improved or reformed. The change is at the inward center; it takes place at the very seat of the conscious life where meaning is focused and motives issue. The needed "inward harmony" for self is found in submission to a new Lord; it is known through surrender to a new authority that is right and righteous and personal. It is this that settles uneasiness, for sin is broken and forgiveness granted.

The chief sin is self-will, rebellion against God by preferring one's own will in opposition to the concerns of God. This self-bent in man is the perversity that plagues the natural self. The only effective and decisive handling of self-will is known through surrender to the authority of Christ. The self then no longer stands apart from, and against, the will of God. The self and God share life in willed togetherness; newness and nearness are thereby realized in the life. The old, sin-bent, selfish life is "put off," discarded as unfit clothes, and the change is evidenced in a moral and spiritual experience.

Paul explains this in Ephesians 4:24, where he speaks about "the new nature, created after the likeness of God in true righteousness and holiness." The near-parallel verse in Colossians 3:10 describes the believer as "renewed in knowledge after the image of its creator." The allusion to Genesis 1:27 (and the parallel at 5:1b) is immediately evident. Scripture citations are abundant to make the point clear that the Christian holds in his life a new pattern of trustworthy data which presents *some higher facts* for scientific study.

The encounter with Jesus Christ grants a new contour and content and character for human experience. With his interior region most radically and redemptively reached, the sentiments, feelings, reasoning, will, and all of what constitutes the inmost self undergo change through his touch. It means that more and more the experiencing man will know himself as a new creature "in Christ." The encounter is far easier to experience than to explain; even the vast supply of psychological terminology of our time is woefully inadequate to explain the Christian condition. But lest this limitation unduly disturb us, let us remember that even the survey of factors in human personality without Christ continues to show how experts remained stumped.

This whole field of human studies unearths such difficulties that Gordon W. Allport, after more than thirty years in studying this field, has lamented, "Personality is far too complex a thing to be trussed up in a conceptual straight jacket."[1] So Wayne E. Oates has rightfully insisted that the Christian "has a contribution to make to psychologist, psychiatrist, and psychoanalyst in the assessment of the *nature* of the encounter whereby man is fundamentally changed and as to the *quality* of selfhood into which he is being changed."[2] If "The self," as Theodore

25

Reik believes, "is still the wealthiest mine of psychological discoveries,"[3] then we must state that the Christian self is increasingly more so. This is a reasonable statement inasmuch as the man who is a Christian self through Christ has found his proper image and identity.

Christian selfhood enhances life in general and grants a higher life in particular. Jesus declared, "I came that they may have life, and have it abundantly" (John 10:-10b). The implications of this bequeathment are much too much for the mind to immediately fathom and totally relate or chart. It is a big event to be confronted and converted. It is an eventful experience whose meanings must unfold across the rest of one's life. *Newness of self is the greatest event possible for any man.* Experience with Christ initiates that newness, and obedient discipleship sustains it. Conformity to Christ means that newness will be determinative, durative, and increasingly developed.

The Christian man knows something in his experience that he did not have before: newness, forgiveness, peace of soul, a singlemindedness. He also finds something strengthened that was weak before: ability to do the right as he understands it. What he is by heredity remains the same, he is still a product of many streams of physical influences, with certain marked traits and capacities. But the Christian now handles them in a new spirit and within a new style of life modeled after the influence of the Christ he believes and follows. His pliable self is at the redemptive disposal of Christ. The perduring agent that is his inner self is now oriented to both life here and life hereafter: The problem of sin is handled by a Greater One. The life of Christ shows the life of God manifested in intimate connection with humanity.

THE CHRISTIAN SELF

The Christian is one who commits himself to progressively know that life through the company of Christ. Taking Christ as his proper image as well as his deliverer, the Christian self will seek to progressively *reflect* the one he follows. And he will also seek to *refract* the Christ less and less. It was a man who had this as his concern who wrote, ". . . it is no longer I who live, but Christ who lives in me; and the life I now live in the flesh I live by faith in the Son of God, who loved me and gave himself for me" (Gal. 2:20*b*). He added, "I do not nullify the grace of God" (2:21*a*).

"The unique factor in Christianity," writes A. Victor Murray, "is that the original experience which brought the religion into being has repeated itself all down the ages, and it is always an experience of the same thing."[4] It is encounter with the person of Christ through his word and Spirit.

---

[1]*Becoming: Basic Considerations for a Psychology of Personality* (New Haven: Yale University Press, 1955), p. vii.
[2]*Christ and Selfhood* (New York: Association Press, 1961), p. 26.
[3]*The Secret Self: Psychoanalytic in Life and Literature* (New York: Grove Press, Inc., 1952 Evergreen Edition, 1960), p. 8.
[4]*Personal Experience and the Historic Faith* (New York: Harper and Brothers, Publishers, 1954), p. 6. See also John E. Smith, *Experience and God* (New York: Oxford University Press, 1968).

2: The Soul Under Siege

The Christian life has to be lived in a wayward world. The common life of the world is corrupt. It does not provide a congenial environment for godly living. There is always a definite contrast between the Christian self and ungodly surroundings; and there is always a conflict between the two.

The Christian must therefore learn how to live with sobriety, uprightness, and godliness in such a world. He must learn to effectively resist what opposes his stand. He must learn to maintain the conduct of his new life. He must learn to develop his newness. He cannot escape the issues of conflict—they are so many and occur on so many levels of experience. But whether social or private, each conflict is serious, fundamental, and involves an evident, unavoidable stress within him. The Christian needs to understand that stress and take proper steps to manage it.

Some years ago the ABC radio network gave two months of Sunday evening broadcasts based upon special presentations from the Cathedral of St. John the Divine, in New York. The presentations were all trialogues, conversations among three voices. Two of the voices represented opposite poles of moral counsel, good versus evil, while the third voice was that of a tempted soul caught between the conflicting crossfire of the other two. That, in short, is the Christian's most pressing problem. It is no small matter when the soul is under stress. When temptation comes, the soul is under siege.

The word "siege" has come into our language through the Old French *sieger,* meaning "to sit." It is a linguistic leftover from the time when the Normans held control of England. It recalls the pattern of intended conquest of a city: an army would settle about a town, shutting it off from outside help, waiting to assault and compel the distressed inhabitants to yield. "Siege" is also a plain word that describes the experience of temptation. One feels caught, held fast, in the middle of a critical and unavoidable test for the self.

It is important to examine the nature of the siege we face and feel. Just what is the character of temptation?

Temptation As Natural Circumstance

Temptation can be considered, first, as a circumstance growing out of our human position. Paul suggested this aspect of meaning in his statement to the believers at Corinth: "No temptation has overtaken you that is not common to man. God is faithful, and he will not let you be tempted beyond your strength, but with the temptation will also provide the way of escape, that you may be able to endure it" (1 Cor. 10:13).

Temptation is common to humanity. It grows out of the open recognition of needs, the assertive urge of some pointed desire, or the awareness of some self-pleasing possibility. Those three factors—needs, desire, possibility —provide the area within which temptation as a natural circumstance takes its rise.

All men are subject to needs. All men know desire. All men are aware of possibility for themselves. Our nature as humans makes us so aware, knowledgeable, and subject. As contingent, dependent creatures, we bear within ourselves the impulse to find and use what will fulfill us.

THE SOUL UNDER SIEGE

Our needs, desires, and possibilities as humans are to be understood basically, as agencies toward our completeness, as means toward that "fulness of life." Our daily pattern of actions is directed toward this end. We begin and end our lives within this common context of concern. The very felt realization of stress when a need is not met, or when a desire is not fulfilled, or when some possibility is sensed—but is not attained—grows, then, out of a natural circumstance. This struggle is therefore common to all men: it is an affliction of life produced by life.

Temptation As a Contrivance

But there is generally more within the experienced siege than natural event and circumstance. The word "temptation" translates a Greek word of wider meaning, *pierasmos*. It is a term of multiple use, sometimes meaning (as we have just seen) a condition of stress that tries us, and sometimes meaning a contrivance of Satan to ruin us. This distinction is pointed out for us in 1 Thessalonians 3:5, where Paul commented: "For this reason, when I could bear it no longer, I sent that I might know your faith, for fear that somehow the tempter had tempted you and that our labor would be in vain."

Or consider 1 Corinthians 7:5, which Paul addressed to the married: "Do not refuse one another except perhaps by agreement for a season, that you may devote yourselves to prayer; but then come together again, lest Satan tempt you through lack of self-control."

Such verses remind us that natural circumstances become anxious occasions for Satan who seeks to render us failures by his besieging work.

THE SOUL UNDER SIEGE

Temptation As Crisis

So then, circumstance is the basis for a contrivance that puts us to the test. The hour of temptation is therefore one of threat and danger. It is dangerous because a lack of steadied intent toward God can permit an ungodly consequence. James 1:13-14 deals with this: "Let no one say when he is tempted, 'I am tempted by God'; for God cannot be tempted with evil and he himself tempts no one. But each person is tempted when he is lured and enticed by his own desire." This problem of unmanaged desire is also pointed out in 1 Timothy 6:9, "But those who desire to be rich fall into temptation, into a snare, into many senseless and hurtful desires that plunge men into ruin and destruction." The soul must be prepared for the time of besiegement. Proper handling of the crisis depends upon a proper handling of the self.

Mark 14:38 gives the word of Jesus about such preparation against failure when temptation comes. "Watch and pray that you may not enter into temptation; the spirit indeed is willing, but the flesh is weak." The scene of the statement is familiar. It was uttered by Jesus in the Garden to the "responsible three"—Peter, James, and John—who relaxed their vigilance in watching for him in order to nap, even as he prayed under strain of a foreseen cross. It was a night of focused besiegement for them all. It was a point of time when the life course of each one was put to the test, subjected to overwhelming peril. But Jesus had prayed and did not alter his purpose under God.

The disciples, on the other hand, did not sense the critical nature of that night at first. When the soldiers came and arrested Jesus, the disciples acted in fear and de-

31

serted him in panic. Under the control of an anxious self-concern, they failed. The overwhelming peril of that occasion had not only involved them but had defeated them. Those men later rallied themselves, but only after an occasion of ruin. These disciples did not have proper hold upon themselves; nor had they prayed—as did Jesus—for God to so hold them.

A felt threat upset those men. Anxiety swamped them and made them victims of confused thought, half-judgments, unreflecting action, and selfish concern. Each man felt what William James has called "the individual pinch of destiny." The whole scene had engulfed the disciples with head-shaking suddenness.

Some situations of stress are clearly marked. They bear open elements that are pointedly evil at first sight. Some other occasions are more subtle in their appearance. The implications of those times steal in upon us unrecognized at first: they come stealthily, unnamed, and unlabeled. A crisis is evident when the full realization seizes us that we have been seized. We feel the pull of the situation. The crisis, then, is not wholly the product of the situation in which one finds himself; it is, in part, a product of the situation he finds *in himself*. Besiegement excites feelings and exacts an attitude. Those feelings must be focused before the soul can be steadied. And steadiness is a must if the struggle is to be won and not lost.

There is generally more to the experience of siege than natural circumstance. Satan acts against us within the struggle. Any study of temptation, then, demands far more than a searching look at ourselves. It also demands a studied look at the person and work of Satan.

"Your adversary the devil!" No authentic theology

bypasses this figure. He is not a mere figure of super-
stition, and his work against man is not indeterminate. His
aims and attitudes are uncovered for us in the light of
revealing Scripture. There are passages there which tell
us that he tempts, that he possesses, that he afflicts, that
he accuses, and that he seeks our ruin. No authentic theology can afford to bypass such a figure.

No man has lived in utter isolation from the work of
this enemy of righteous living. There are many things we
do not know about him. We speculate on the details sur-
rounding his present state and possible past, trying with
intent to grasp some loose end for the sake of logic. We
do not know all about him, but we do know his work.

We know his work from biblical revelation. We also
know it from within our own suggestive struggles while
under siege. Paul Tillich tells us that he visited his friend
David Roberts a few days before Roberts died, and he
heard him—with insight into his sickness—say, "If I ever
should become healthy again, I will be able to say what the
demonic is." Every alert soul can add his own personal
word to the account. The "dimension of the demonic"
is more than a technical topic in theology. The agitation
we suffer at the hands of our spiritual adversary (see 1
Peter 5:8) is a very real matter.

Time magazine once carried a report about a complaint
made to some Anglican bishops against changing certain
words in the Church of England catechism. The catechism
begins with the question: "What did your godparents
promise for you at your baptism?" Across the centuries
those instructed for confirmation have had to give this
required answer: "I would renounce the devil and all his
work." A revision commission had proposed to strike out

all mention of the devil, dropping the designation in an effort to be in agreement with modern thought. But complaints were too numerous against the proposed change. And her version was submitted by the committee to the responsible bishops, reading: "I would renounce the devil and fight against evil." One of the committee members admitted that the word "devil" gives people "a better idea of what they're up against."

The artists of the Middle Ages depicted the devil as a ludicrous creature, foul, and inexpressibly ugly. They rather mirrored his life, not his looks. They suggested his unequaled sin and the ghastly nature of his work. No man lives in isolation from him. When temptation comes, we are all reminded of "what [we're] up against."

But what is his point? The question is certainly in order. The answer can be brief and pointed: our adversary works against us in envy. Every person rightly related to God has something that he has lost. Everything has possibilities of restoration and upward progression except our adversary. "Whosoever will" can have a future with God, but not our adversary. He is out to disrupt that possible end open to every man. He is intent to make all others share his misery. Nothing enhances his life; nothing mitigates his misery. His point is determined by his own personhood—to make all others like himself. And that is what we must fight against when we are besieged by him.

Just how does the devil act against us? What are his most obvious strategems? We have already observed that he has to work within the confines of our human circumstance. He *meets* us where we *find* ourselves. Situations are his province of operation. Stress is his working moment. Suggestion is his tempting tool.

THE SOUL UNDER SIEGE

Let us examine these in more detail.

1. *Situations.* Situations are Satan's province of operation against us. The situations he exploits are many and varied, too numerous for a full accounting here. There is the situation of poverty, with all its attendant pressures. The resources are inadequate, and the sense of security is always but a desire. There is the situation of having riches, and the corresponding concern to retain, use, and increase them—without loss. There is the time of sickness: when the personal life is disrupted and the expenses mount, making the whole pattern of life undergo drastic revisions. There is the pressured situation of strained human relations, marital difficulties, broken friendships, social problems because of a stand taken on an issue. Some persons are caught in the situation of teen-age changes. Some others are in their older years, beset with fears of what a shift of status might mean; they do not welcome the inevitable slowing of pace. The frequent lapses of memory unsettle them; and, to a deeper extent, the loss by death of close friends of many years distresses them.

The list of situations could well continue, for life is still wider and our problems still more personal. But every situation is personal. It is heavy and sharp. It cuts and disturbs at deep levels. Paul has well put it, "We are afflicted in every way . . . perplexed . . . persecuted . . . struck down . . ." (2 Cor. 4:8-9). Our adversary seeks us out at such moments and intensifies our struggles by his threatening work. He meets us *in extremis* and tries to goad us to extremes.

2. *Stress.* The time of our stress is Satan's prized working moment. We realize the presence of stress whenever a power that is opposite to our intent makes us strain in our

THE SOUL UNDER SIEGE

efforts. Our normal reaction is to reduce the strain as much as possible. When we are besieged, however, there is that God-ordained escape that must be found. According to 2 Corinthians 10:13, there is a proper way out of the stress. Although the struggle makes us feel spent, we are enabled to fight until we win release as victors, however absorbing and demanding the experience.

The struggle of some Christians appears harder to be handled because they become depressed during the siege of their soul. The previous bliss of belonging to Christ becomes overshadowed by the cloud of conflict with their adversary. The mood is certainly not one of exhilaration but of extremity. The pull of the whole experience upon the inward self tends to crush. Spontaneity is strangely absent. Freedom then seems more like a curse than like a complement. There is the wish that God would guarantee the moment for the soul. It is the experience of so many persons that the austerity of the stress settles depressingly upon their minds. And then it does not *feel* like the joy of the Lord is their strength. Such depression can be a real foe to needed steadiness while under siege.

Depression is another lingering evidence of our acute sensitivity as creatures in a world of change. Martin Luther confessed his sensitivity to depression. His melancholia has been the subject of many learned volumes by students of his life. There were times, his biographers tell us, when depression was so heavy upon Luther that his reason and will seemed diseased. He waged a perpetual battle for faith. Luther felt inwardly bankrupt, completely abandoned for long periods over several years. At times he felt so beaten and mauled by depression that he was more aware of his depression than he was of God or faith. The most severe upheaval of his life along this line came in 1527. He stated that for more than a week he was close to the gates of death and hell. "I trembled in all my members," he confessed. He felt both distance and despair.

Luther later learned that many of those seasons of depression were Satan-induced. He even said that the devil talked with him, in quite direct terms. He learned, however, how to handle the matter. "Don't argue with the devil. He has had five thousand years of experience. He has tried out all of his tricks on Adam, Abraham, and David, and he knows exactly the weak spots."

Luther's weak spot was the tendency to be depressed. That tendency to depression is certainly for many others one of those weak spots. It is of interest to note, however, that it was in that same year of 1527 that Luther composed his stirring hymn of trust, "A Mighty Fortress Is Our God."

Depression can be handled. It does not have to turn us over to a besieging devil. There is a meaning for the soul that is deeper than any mood. Our hope is rooted in faith. Depression is a dangerous mood, to be sure, but it is only a mood. A mood can rob us of previous feeling, but it need not rob us of spiritual fact. Salvation is deeper than a mood.

A friend was telling me some time ago about his major bout with depression. He had suffered a major disappointment in his marriage. He was in college at the time it all happened. He felt like leaving school but had steadied himself sufficiently to remain. His mind had its foggy days. Howard Thurman came to the campus for a week of lectures. The student (graduate) had met Dr. Thurman on another occasion and thus met with him to renew the friendship. He also shared his problem with that wise and alert leader. Thurman's counsel was unforgettable. After being told *when* the experience had taken place and that the friend had managed to bear up *since,* Thurman told him (and note the approach!):

"You have missed a wonderful opportunity to fold up! When you would have collapsed, you didn't. From what you say you have won the battle and you have the victory. Now you are still on the top of the heap. Don't take that victory and throw it away because of a mood!"

The thrust was wise indeed. Moods can be dangerous, if we yield under the aggravation they impose. But salvation is deeper than any mood. The victorious change we have witnessed will remain when the moods all pass, if we do not yield when the moods linger.

Discouragement can also aggravate the time of stress. Most of us remember that oft-told allegory about Satan holding council with his demon-agents concerning a soul they were trying to ensnare. Previous efforts had failed to lure the man from God. The man's case history was recited. Each imp told what he had tried against the man, but all had failed. One alert imp rose and spoke forth in hasty confidence, "I will make him sin!" "And by what means?" Satan queried. "Ha!" the imp ventured, after listening to all the previously-tried methods. "I will go and discourage him!" The whole council was pleased at the idea. Satan commended the imp on his wisdom. Discouragement in the midst of stress has robbed many persons of the strength needed to maintain their stand against the devil.

The chain of strategems used by Satan is longer still. There is depression, despair, discouragement. There is also

THE SOUL UNDER SIEGE

self-pity. He who yields the struggle through self-pity abandons his Savior for the sake of his self. Running from the struggle, he falls into the waiting arms of the adversary. He who indulges in self-pity only salutes his sadness and fattens selfishness. Self-pity is a purpose-denying mood. Life is no longer understood as a purpose but as a problem.

From Chinese literature a story has come to us about a man who leaned too far over the edge of his boat one night to kiss his image in the reflected moonlight on the water and fell to his death by drowning. The soul that pities itself while under siege also leans too far. He leans to kiss himself, trying to give himself the security and warmth he thinks God has denied him. He falls and loses his spiritual life in the waters of selfishness.

While visiting a public library one night, I was attracted to a book on the works of Schopenhauer. I had just read a few lines of the introduction by Will Durant, which included, "Every man knows, and every woman too, that the years bring a rich assortment of pains and sorrows to every soul; and that life is still a precious thing only because the joys it gives are deep enough to be worth all the price we pay." I stopped at that point. I had to stop, because some earlier reader of that book had penciled a star where that sentence ended and had scribbled a footnote at the bottom of the page. It said: "*Critical Footnote: Suppose it doesn't bring any joys?"

Some person's life had erupted at the point of that line. The added footnote was emotion charged. Some bitter experience had caused that question to rise. Some unresolved rough spot in life had laid hands on that soul. I still wonder whether that disturbed person has ever passed on from that experience of pain to know the saving person Jesus Christ, who brings to every believer "the joy of the Lord."

There are times when the flavor of life grows bitter. All men have known the inner cry, even those who in stoic reserve shed no outward tear. When life grows bitter to the taste, there is the temptation to retaliate against life by becoming inwardly bitter. Life is always relentless in its demands upon us all to adjust, to adjust rapidly and repeatedly. The time of adjustment is a time of stress. What a person does as a method of adjustment forms an index to what he really believes about life and about God. Adjustment to the questions raised by life—suffering being one of them—will either be cowardly or creative.

The coward flies in escape, in one way or another— usually a self-pity of retreat. The creative soul focuses attention to fill his need and reaches beyond himself to gain godly help for his life. The Christian is such a soul. His help is not in mere mental reserve; he is given godly strength in the midst of his stress. He faces the matter and seeks to steady himself. Once he passes through the valley of the shadowed siege, he raises a song in the interest of his triumph. All men suffer. All men sing. It is the content of the song that tells the one's faith or the other's sense of fate. We will either sing in honor of our blessings or mirror our humanity in our "blues."

The aggravation of the stress is most pointed because we feel it as a *suffering individual*. The time of besiegement is a time of highly individual feeling. The inward state is greatly intensified. The field of awareness narrows to consider mainly one's own self. The sense of self is attacked and the sense of freedom is put under tension. The occasion seems full and final—and deadly. There is both incitement and excitement. The feelings are varied at first; then they become centered in order to either resist or receive. This "moment of aroused freedom" is no simple moment.

All men know such stress. All men know some kind of situation in which they have felt the demands of that stress. Some become depressed in the experience. Some are discouraged in the testing. Some yield to self-pity and act in sinful selfishness. But stress does not need to mean completed seduction of soul.

The Christian is intent to resist the adversary who aggravates the stress in the siege. Important to that resistance is the knowledge (and the remembrance) that the whole experience is only "common to man." No temptation, then, is to be considered unusual; and no temptation is really new. There are only the same old situations involving new persons. Each person must learn how to handle the stress those occasions bring. Each person must be prepared against the adversary who works in that stress.

If the struggles of our souls were as openly told as they are intimately known, the similarity of our sufferings would be so great as to forbid forever the feeling that we are alone in them, or that one's life is filled with unique problems known only by oneself. As to our differences of experience—what are those felt differences except timing or intensity? or perhaps duration? Sometimes the differences are in the outcome.

All men know temptation, but not all handle it the same. The Christian is intent to handle it after the set manner of Jesus when the trouble comes.

THE SOUL UNDER SIEGE

3. *Suggestion*. Suggestion is Satan's tempting tool. He makes suggestions in order to lure the soul into sin.

I have stated above that the devil meets us where we find ourselves. In his attempt to incite desire, his intent is to lure us to where we are not. In the face of felt needs he offers suggestions that sting. Like us, he has appraised our felt problem; but he has done so with a fiendish mentality and intent. Knowing the stress we feel, he colors the whole issue in his own way and makes available some "solution" to the matter. The offer comes with strict timing, leveled at the very area where we *know* the problem keenest. Suggestion aggravates the crisis to a more than considerable extent. The appeal is made by something of promise. This in turn only aggravates and deepens the pathos of the incompleteness we feel. We are filled with care and want the disorder removed; we want the need met; we want the uneasiness settled. The devil suggestively *shows* a way.

It is the fact that we humans tend to be troubled more so about what is not with us than about what is with us. It is reported that a friend of Charles Dickens gave him a gift, a silver centerpiece. A letter arrived with the gift, explaining why a certain piece from the original design was missing. The design represented the four seasons of the year. The letter explained that the winter figure, being dull and drab, would be out of character of Dickens, his friend having known him as bright and gay of mood. But Dickens afterward remarked that he could never look at the gift without thinking about winter. A memory had him disturbed. A knowledge of what was missing centered his attention—quite involuntarily at first—upon the fact that it *was* missing. His sense of order and balance was beset. Something unfinished always prods us to see it finished.

THE SOUL UNDER SIEGE

And that is the situation of our lives. We are essentially unfinished. Our adversary appeals to this fact with suggestive offers for solving any problem we face, intent to trap us if we act upon any one of them.

Self-planning never leads to completeness where moral and spiritual issues are at stake. Self-planning only leads us to sin, which is rather a confinement of life, because he who sins restricts himself to the circle of his own selfish concerns. He becomes and remains a victim on the spiral of self-centered living.

Only out of the knowledge and conviction of this truth can a man break the circle of self-centered living. It is only when that circle is broken that such a man learns the freedom of the righteous act. He then transcends himself in the fulfillment of obedience to God. He no longer sees life in a perspective that shows himself as the center. Rather, he sees Jesus Christ as the center of the new meaning for his life. Nor can he afterward hold an easy view regarding sin. He sees sin as a self-asserting, God-defying act. The Christian man is intent to stand "against the wiles of the devil . . . to withstand in the evil day, and having done all, to stand" (Eph. 6:11, 13).

Yes, we are unfinished. Our recurring needs and ever-present sense of our possibilities are instant reminders. The circumstances of our needs and our desires furnish ground upon which self-concern inevitably operates. Our adversary seeks to make us so anxious about our state that we will be willing to accept his solicitations. The Christian man is intent to steady himself against the pressures of those felt beckonings. He refuses to obey the voice of the tempter. The Christian keeps himself for God.

THE SOUL UNDER SIEGE

The Christian's resolve to keep himself will be tested and retested again and again. The siege of the soul does not end after a suggestion has been spurned. If *allurement* fails to trap us, the adversary uses *accusation:* he will seek to confuse us by the reactions we feel when under siege, charging us—true to his character as Satan—that we have not really been changed within! The charge is against our temperament, saying that it is still sinful because of its reaction to the thing offered us in suggestive promise. Satan charges that because the personal center of concern was so touched, the very reaction could only be sin. As an operation which takes place within the self this whole matter of how temptation is to be distinguished from actual sin can be very disturbing and confusing.

There is a scene in *The Pilgrim's Progress* that deals with this. Christian was moving through a place of strange sights and sounds, a place of disorder and dread. He had a cautious concern and a drawn sword as he moved along. There were voices all around him. At one point he heard so much from those voices that he wondered whether he himself had said some of what he was hearing. Some wicked fiend had managed to get so close to Christian's ear that the suggestions he offered seemed to issue from Christian's own mind. It was so dark and discouraging a state that Christian "had not the discretion either to stop his ears, or to know from whence those blasphemies came." It was only when a higher and more powerful word came from "the voice of a man, as going before him," —the voice of Jesus—that Christian was steadied in mind though still in the midst of dangers.

The resolute Christian will have such a stratagem used against him. And since this particular wile is one of the

THE SOUL UNDER SIEGE

most puzzling of all the wiles of Satan, it is important here to trace out the human ground upon which the adversary seeks to confuse and condemn the Christian who has refused his beckonings.

The Devil an Observer

The biblical record suggests that the devil is an eager observer of human life. A scene from the story of Job shows the devil busy "going to and fro in the earth, and from walking up and down in it" (Job 1:7), presumably studying the concerns and ways of men. The story of Job even shows us that the devil's observations make him presume to predict a man's behavior under a given set of circumstances, that a man will sin—and in a certain manner of evil—if put under particular stress. Again and again the devil tried to predict Job's "weak spot" but failed.

The biblical record also shows us times when the devil did not fail in his attempts to cause human failure. In every such instance he appealed to each man's self-concern, his chosen scheme of life, his traits, attitudes, past experiences. He used just that strategy of influence that appeared to him best suited in that man's case.

The structure and dynamics of the inner life are not unknown to our adversary. He has watched us in our living and has gained an alertness regarding our dreams and ambitions, our successes and failures, our acts of wisdom and deeds of folly. He knows that all of these have affected us, that they have registered in that interior region that houses all the life we have lived. The devil has long known what psychologists are pointing out with increasing concern: that all of our experiences stand mysteriously mingled somewhere within us, and that we are the province of a mind that plans and a wider self that reacts. All that we have lived is linked within us, particularly on the level of memory. Since this is so, a calculated touching of the mind can sometimes bring about a kind of "all-over" reaction; the body then shares in what the mind sees, reacting to the stab of that sensation.

"Impressions of past experience should not be regarded too lightly," we have been advised by psychiatrists, "whether the person was fully aware of the entire import of what was happening or not. Most of the wisest and most of the most foolish things we do in our lives, we do as the result of present impressions associated in our minds with many other past experiences and our former methods of reacting to them, rather than carefully thought-out planning." This is certainly pertinent to our discussion of temptation and sin. The suggested thing is offered by Satan. We see and recognize it for what it is—a thing offered by Satan. We refuse it. But the reaction of the self in the midst of the anxiety we felt during the offer is seized upon by Satan as a sinful expression. Satan knows that we are confused by this because past responses stand mirrored to us when we see the thing before us. What we have previously known and done tends to rise within the memory; definite associations are made—all without our immediate consent. The memory and imagination have been triggered quite involuntarily. The fact that there is often an "overall response" further aggravates the stress.

THE SOUL UNDER SIEGE

Power of Suggestion

Here again we see the crucial nature of suggestion. Suggestion carries a great weight of authority, touching the strain of the curiosity within us, while giving data for the work of imagination. Suggestion also taps the memory and brings before us from the past any associations that we have known with the situation in question. All of this can take place without our consent. To the extent that these associations and memories come involuntarily, to that extent Satan is still trying to manipulate our behavior. To the extent that we censor the offered scene and data, demanding order on the basis of the new life and law of Christ, to that extent we have again resisted the tempter. One is reminded here of the word of Clarence Irving, "What we shall think *of,* is partly within our control and partly not; but what we shall think *of it* is our full responsibility."

The questionable aspects of the "overall response" must be considered against that background explanation. Temptation, we have said, is not wholly the product of the situation in which one finds himself, but also is in part a product of the situation one finds *in* himself. When temptation comes, we always bring to the experience something more than what was originally there: we bring with us our past, however full or empty it was, and thus the whole time of temptation is colored by what we have previously known, experienced, and lived. To the extent that we have lived, to that extent our memory stands available to be touched upon by a similar scene or circumstance. This reaction does not show that sin has taken place but rather that memories so involve us that they can stimulate us upon return. Those memories are not confined to the mind but are felt as well in the body. Memory and anxiety both have such affective power.

Memory and the Brain

Some quite revealing studies along this line have been made available to the world through the researches of Dr. Wilder Penfield, a man noted for his work in neurology and neurosurgery. Dr. Penfield is founder of the Montreal Neurological Institute and a leading brain specialist. Curious about how the mind works and how the brain performs its distinctive functions, Dr. Penfield devoted several years to some basic explorations and became the first man to activate brain nerve cells from outside and make them respond to direct manipulation.

The human brain is wrinkled and gray in color. The grayness is the color of a kind of mantle that grows on the top of the brain as its cover. This cover is called the cerebral cortex. The covering continues to grow throughout the years; thus the wrinkles. The cortex contains countless nerve cells. All of them are in touch with each other and in touch and tune with the rest of the nervous system of the entire body. It has been discovered that all human sensations and all human movement are controlled by various sections of the cortex. In seeking to know just what particular parts of the cortex control or supply impulses for thought, feeling, and motion, Dr. Penfield has supplied the world with some amazing information.

In a certain surgical case he applied a gentle electric shock to an exposed part of the patient's brain. By this he found that he stimulated the movement of an arm, then a leg. He stimulated a part of one of the temporal lobes and thereby chanced upon the storehouse of that patient's memories. When his electric needle gave shock to that area of the brain the patient began to recall an incident long-since forgotten.

In another case, Dr. Penfield was operating on the brain of a young woman who had been an epileptic. When he stimulated a certain section of her brain surface, she began to tell him that she was hearing an orchestra playing a song. Penfield switched the power off from his needle; the song stopped. The song returned in the young woman's mind when Dr. Penfield turned the power in his needle on again. Interestingly, the young woman said the song sounded within with the same force and clarity as when she first heard it years previously. The song went on from verse to verse, the chorus included, and at tempo. A whole event, indelibly recorded years before in her brain, was being tapped again and drawn from some microscopic cells of her temporal lobe. And all of this was quite involuntary to her intent. Her memory center was being stimulated by a means other than her own intent to recall.

The moment of temptation also involves the tapping of one's memory center. Without any concern to recall or imagine, we are made aware of what stands before the consciousness. Calculated suggestions bring all this about. It is true that such effects of remembered sin can give one a sense of *feeling* soiled—even when he has resisted the suggestion to sin itself. The very vividness of detail does tend to sap strength, saddle the mind, and ride the will with an accusing weight. The whole matter seems so much a part of the self that the question inevitably rises as to whether one has really been made anew within by Christ.

THE SOUL UNDER SIEGE

In the light of the discussion given above, one must recognize the effects of suggestion for what they are: intended elements toward the manipulation of our lives by the devil. If he cannot muddy the life, Satan will then try to muddle the mind, confuse against self-containment, deny the essential experience of conversion, and accuse one of having sinned by reaction. Lacking control over the Christian's conscious intent, Satan seeks to rule by subconscious reactions. It is all his attempt to manipulate our behavior from other levels of the self, to rope in the mind and make it victim by exciting our emotions through memory. It is a last measure of evil to finally coerce us.

Temptation and Sin

Thus the sharpness of the experience. No symbol is unimportant and no feeling remains out-of-bounds or untouched. The whole self is involved when temptation comes. The whole self knows stress when the soul is under siege. What we see, we sense. What we feel seems what we are *totally*.

But it is not fully so. There is no sin involved in being tempted until the *suggested* evil becomes the *accepted* evil. W. E. Sangster has treated this theme with characteristic wisdom and insight in his study on Christian sanctity, *The Pure in Heart*. He wrote: "Temptation becomes sin when the self is identified with it. As life bubbles out of the subconscious, it bubbles out raw: amoral: just animal life. It were best to regard it as no more than instinct and 'reaction' at this stage. The moot question, 'What can grace do for the subconscious?' requires for an answer that we bear in mind that God treats us always as persons. . . . The high distinctiveness of the saint in his mastery of self is here: that, as his yeasting life rises out of the subconscious, he assesses every desire and aspiration instantly in the pure presence of God and identifies himself for or against it, according to that swift assessment made in the light of heaven. What God approves, he pursues. What God condemns, he spurns."*

We never lose what we live. However, we are as Christians changed from what we were. Scenes from a stirred memory can pull, push, or plague us. But guilt is not based by God on a stirred memory, nor the presence of a question mark in the mind, but on conscious intent in wrongdoing. Suggestive elements will touch us but they do not have to trap and ruin us. Satan knows that we enter each moment of life with a memory and curiosity that are parts of our basic, personal equipment for life. By his stratagems, he manipulates them as agents for our spiritual death. Like Paul, "we are not ignorant of his designs" (2 Cor. 2:11); nor are we powerless against them.

It is always in the power of the Christian to censor the scene of his siege, demand order within himself, and take his stand upon the given Word of God. He is under necessity only to follow what is the will of God. Knowing this, he can bring his remembered past under the management of grace and God's *remembered* will. The Christian can responsibly act in faith and strength to, "destroy arguments and every proud obstacle to the knowledge of God, and take every thought captive to obey Christ," as Paul put it (2 Cor. 10:5). The Christian can order his life because of an ordained principle and power of action through the internal work of the abiding Spirit

*Nashville: Abingdon Press, 1955, p. 234.

3: The Christian Stance

The Christian is concerned to guard his attention and intent during times of stress. He must therefore hold a certain stance of soul. He must set himself to act properly when under siege. He must, in short, stay ready for life.

Ready for life is a crucial phrase! I shall never forget how I thought about this concern as I stood one afternoon some years ago in the Museum of Egyptian Antiquities in Cairo, Egypt. Our tour group was being shown the sumptuous furniture pieces, fans, shields, jewels, and relics from the tomb of Tut-Ankh-Amen. The objects had been excavated after his royal tomb had been found intact, left strangely unfound by would-be plunderers for about three thousand years.

I was especially impressed by the display of two statues of the dead king. Each one was a recognizable likeness, painted to display his youthful elegance and physical characteristics. The guide explained the purpose of the two statues: they had been placed in the tomb as guards, stationed just outside the funerary chambers as wardens for the dead king's body and soul. Upon hearing this, my thought soared—even in death the king wanted constant guard over himself. Prepared in his likeness, the two statues represented the king's own guard over himself. He had sought to make personal provision for his own welfare, placing himself under double guard. Armed with mace and staff, each statue was poised for defensive action.

It is rather the living soul that needs to be guarded. But the responsibility is certainly personal. George Heath has

THE CHRISTIAN STANCE

captured this insight with his pen, charging himself, "My Soul, Be on Thy Guard":

> *My soul, be on thy guard;*
> *Ten thousand foes arise;*
> *The hosts of sin are pressing hard*
> *To draw thee from the skies.*

The charge is toward readiness for life.

The Christian stance is a will strongly set for righteous living. It is a determination to be godly. It is a will disposed toward the will of God. The stance begins at conversion—that conversion of heart and life which took place only after we decided to turn our will toward God's will for us. No man ever drifts into a righteous life. He must enter by direct decision and intent. He must enter through the promptings of grace and the clear light of saving truth. So then: when the Christian's stance is threatened, he continues to act out of the decision he originally made in the sight of God. He keeps himself by the same set of mind and heart to which he became committed.

This matter of decision is central in a continued Christian experience. All proper action is in terms of it. The decision gave God freedom to savingly handle the sinful past. The continued decision grants him freedom to shape both one's present and future. The call to "repent" was addressed to us in our freedom and need to decide. When we did decide, the decision became the pivot for the saving work of God within us. We retain the new set of soul by the same fixed judgment. When moods grip us, with all the irrationality they bring, it is that decision which remains the pivot upon which our personal response swings toward God in faith and hope and love. His grace gives steadiness to maintain our choice.

Decision: conversion was not possible without it. Continuance with Christ demands that it remain fixed. All failure under stress must be traced back to a breakdown of the will to obey God. There will either be firmness or failure on our part. The decided will is our personal instrument of action before God. It is the organized, dominant thrust that grants us needed position. A decided will binds together the inward forces of our lives for our intended end. When a man has set his will toward the pleasure of God he has taken the vital stance to be ready for life.

Aids for the Will

Making the decision is *our* part. But we all know that man needs something more than sheer will to match life and evil. There is a line in Martin Luther's hymn "A Mighty Fortress Is Our God" which tells the limitation of our self-intent against evil: "Did we in our own strength confide, / our striving would be losing." There are demands in life that exact more of us than sheer will and decision can effectively handle. A decided will only sets us *for* God; God must grant power to effect what the will has approved. We need aids for our will. Mere decision is insufficient except when strengthened by divine gifts.

There is a story in the works of Xenophon about a young Grecian who was so intent to win a chariot race that he added horse after horse to the chariot in an effort to guarantee sufficient means for his intent. He ended with eight fiery steeds pulling the chariot. Our basic willingness to remain righteous is like that chariot: it needs help.

THE CHRISTIAN STANCE

A cartoon pictured two men marooned on an isolated island. They had begun work toward escape by building a boat. The skeleton of the boat was in the picture: one of the men was on top, hammering away; some distance from the project the second man was standing beside a deforested area with an axe in his hand. He yelled out to his hammering companion, "Hold it, Sam! We've run out of timber." They had gone their limit. They had acted— and with worthy intent. The problem still remained, however. Those men could only wait for help from outside. The will open toward God is only a will. It can be set by decision but God must strengthen and equip that will by divine gifts before it can function with full effect and due results. The Christian stance demands a continued action of will between God and man.

Both this concept of "will" and the biblical concept of "sanctification" have been under careful review and discussion in recent years. As for the will, there has been the concern to know and properly articulate the real freedom and powers of the will. Some of the main questions have been: What influences or controls the will? What can it really control? What are the processes by which a man's will informs or asserts itself? Why are some persons so unproductive and unskillful in willing for themselves? Why are some other persons presumably unable to handle themselves or set their will with decisive intent?

As for sanctification, there has been a strong concern to assess what it is, what the means are that effect and sustain it, and what state and effects are to be experienced when sanctification is realized. Some crucial questions about sanctification continue to be: Just how does sanctification affect the disposition? How many substantial changes should be expected in the sanctified self? How do mistakes in judgment, personality quirks, and personal immaturity fit into being made "perfect"? How does biblical perfection relate to the self one knows himself to be?

All these questions about will and sanctification are important. The alert Christian asks such questions with reference to his own life in Christ. He asks because he knows that the continuation of Christ's gifts to him should mean moral and dispositional effects within him. He knows that something definite and delivering took place in his will during the experience of repentance and conversion. He knows that he has changed his mind, turning in full to the God who confronted him in the truth he heard and acknowledged. He knows that he has accepted and adopted God's view of his sinful past, that he has renounced that past and opened himself to the future bestowed by Christ. He knows that he has a new standing in life and before God.

The Christian also realizes that his stand needs to be strengthened and, if possible, guaranteed. It is the participant Holy Spirit who does that strengthening by a sanctifying of the will. The Holy Spirit engages the will in conviction, regenerates the will in conversion, and invests it with a God-ward tendency in sanctification, giving it tone, training, and concern for the practical use of truth for life. "Sanctify them in the truth," Jesus prayed, "thy word is truth" (John 17:17). A renewal of self is initiated in conversion; the repentant man is thus freed to be for Christ. In sanctification the will is strengthened in what becomes a disposition to be for Christ.

Let us be clear in our minds about that province of

THE CHRISTIAN STANCE

self where sanctification is realized. "Will" is the personal power of a man to determine his own actions and effect them. It is the ability to bring all of his experiences and powers into focus in a free and present act of self. This ability involves the man's freedom, motivation, intention, and sense of understanding (or lack of it). Scripture throughout asserts the primacy of reason and will in all human actions. We are creatures whose needs, thoughts, feelings, wishes, desires, circumstances, and possibilities affect the deliberate choices we make in using ourselves. We "will" when something is thought, sensed, realized, scrutinized, and resolved as our attitude or intended action. Will has to do, then, with the consent or dissent of the self in the wake of some realized impulse, image, insight, impression, inclination, or incitement. "Will" is the self focused to act. Usually there is a sense of values, alternatives, and a considered goal.

Christian experience is a willed experience. It does not begin nor continue apart from our consent. The Christian always participates in the quality of his involvement with life, and in the quality of his development as a new self. It is only by consent that we conform to the image of Christ; just as it is only by dissent that we remain opposed to the beckoning pull of the old life of sin. In the humanity of Jesus, we can see what is possible for our own life under God. Although there are ultimacies in Christ that are not in us, watching Christ does make us aware of what is actual for us in terms of moral sensitivity, ethical reflectiveness, spiritual dependence, steadiness of will, and outgoing love for others. Some of these basic ingredients of the sanctified life combine with a host of other ingredients to comprise a God-disposed self.

THE SOUL UNDER SIEGE

The ability to change or alter the new life remains: being free, a man can always turn from God. But when the will is continually open to the participant Helper from God, this stance of godwardness becomes customary, making the whole self progressively realize growth in grace and conformity to Christ. It can be rightly said that the fruit of the Spirit is nothing more nor less than the actualizing in our lives of the dispositional qualities and traits of Jesus himself.

Christian experience is really an involvement between the self and Christ that both will. It is a relationship that is best described as an ellipse with two foci, free consent of the self and necessary conformity to God's known will.

It is by what the self wills that we express the history we approve and wish to initiate and continue. The Christian self finds fulfillment and development between these two real poles of concern: individual freedom and divine call. These comprise the most basic environment for the growing soul. It is the rightful position for growth in obedience and the learning of fidelity to trust. This was the case with Jesus as divine Son. As the writer to the Hebrews stated it, "Although he was a Son, he learned obedience through what he suffered" (5:8). It was the practice of Jesus to invest himself freely, fully, responsibly, in the known will of God for his life. In so doing he did not lose himself; he used himself.

Investing the will is the Christian's proper exercise of soul; it is his utter action as an "individual," as Kierkegaard was wont to insist. The title of one of his most edifying discourses has stressed for all time a central issue for the intent believer: "Purity of Heart Is to Will One

THE CHRISTIAN STANCE

Thing." Christian life demands the recognition of two focuses, not one. It calls upon us to recognize that the believer has to act and respond as a free individual before God, investing himself with concerned will. It also calls upon us to recognize the eternal demands of the will of God. Life with those two concerns in full and responsible view is Christian experience. Both belong to the believer, and obedience is not repression but self-in-action-of-investment-by-call-and-trust. Obedience is never repression; it is the will set free for *becoming*.

There are times when any Christian could wish that right living could be an automatic result, something learned once and lived forever thereafter. But there is some reason and wisdom in the fact that this is not possible for us. If this were so, then in some sense our acts—lacking in *present will*—would be other than continued consent to God.

I was for some years training for the concert stage. I recall giving piano concerts and playing music that was somewhat automatically handled. I say "somewhat automatically handled" because the details of finger change and hand movements, pressure changes on the keys at various points that needed to be shaded for effect, *et al,* all these things had been learned once and for all. The fingers went to work, following the learned path and patterns, and the results showed themselves as my memory-store did its proper work.

But there had to be something more than memory at work. There had to be a supervising agency within to superintend the memory, to make sure that the result was not mechanical, but creative. Consciousness had to be applied lest a wooden performance result. Then, too, consciousness had to doublecheck memory lest mistakes be made. Then, again, tiredness of a hand or wrist needed to be overcome or overborne by conscious process, lest pain ruin the needed coordination. Conscious as well as unconscious factors must forever work in any human undertaking, bringing together value and act, creativity and service, self and contribution.

The value of this continued situation for the self cannot be overemphasized. The body must learn its place under a superintending mind which has been filled with value judgments and principles. Christian experience is a particular kind of experience; it requires particular kinds of actions, and particular channeling of possibilities, a specialized kind of openness to life, and a particualrized handling of life both within and outside one's own self. The conditions of humanity can be learned once and for all, but the exact handling of self in the midst of those conditions must always be fresh and consciously done. This is partly because every new experience pinches the soul in fresh fashion. It is also because nothing creative takes place unless the self is open to it in fresh ways. That is the nature of life; Christian life is not excepted.

Sanctification and the Person

Sanctification has to be discussed, then, in the light of the role of will in our living. The reality of sanctification involves the will in special fashion, infusing it by divine Presence, investing it with a sense of participating Help (Rom. 8:26), and involving it in a responsible freedom. The person will not become mature in a leap but by progressive stages. The person might still be greatly influenced by previous experiences and notions and customs. But within the sphere of sanctification, that person can consciously deal with the leftover deposits from the past in order to be reinformed, redirected, and retrained. Here again we see the importance of realized truth to the development of the Christian's life. We are what we have lived. Just as a sinner has a future in Christ, so does the Christian have a past without Christ.

But the sanctified man—the believer who fully accepts God's choice of him for divine will—can accept himself as he is and, at the same time, act with God upon himself as he sees room for improvement while watching Christ. He does not punish himself for *being short* of what he sees in Jesus. But one proof of sanctification is the will never to rest content in that shortness. The sanctification of the will encourages and enables a man forever to seek the perfection of Christ. It would be a mistake, however, to become morbidly perfectionistic, centered upon the self more than upon God in Christ. The proper stress is upon the granted ability to remain open for willed change in the light of Christ. It is not what is *taken out* of man that counts most for the sanctified life. It is what is *granted* and *placed at our disposal* to be like Christ.

The Gift of Faith

1. The will also finds aid in the gift of *faith*. Faith grants a determined thrust to the will illumined by the Word. At the center of personal concern, faith gathers the self under an informed will; it centers the action as personal, and the attitude of affirmation is the hand by which the decided will grips the purpose of God with surety.

THE SOUL UNDER SIEGE

Such faith is for our total life with all its levels and problems. Paul likened faith to a Roman soldier's shield. "Above all," he exhorted, "taking the shield of faith, with which you can quench all the flaming darts of the evil one" (Eph. 6:16). In using this figure, Paul asserts that faith is both a protective and a pioneering instrument. Like the shield, faith shows its value only as it is in use. Paul used a Greek word for "shield" in that verse which should not escape our notice: the term is *thureos,* a shield used for heavy infantry fighting. It was large-sized, about three feet by four feet, and its user could be entirely protected when in a crouching position. The thrust of this point is unmistakable. Faith is for the whole man, granting protection and centeredness to take any stress. With faith, a decided will can face the whole of life.

Our individual struggles under stress affect the whole self. Faith is of value at such times, for faith claims the whole self for God, allied with a quite determined will, and acting as its primary agent. This faith, this expectancy of spirit, is not of our own making. It follows a prompting word from God. "So faith comes from what is heard, and what is heard comes by the preaching of Christ" (Rom. 10:17). No stance of will can be weak that lives in company with faith, for "faith is the assurance of things hoped for, the conviction of things not seen" (Heb. 11:1).

The Strength of Fear

2. The will finds strengthening nurture in a *fear* governed by the grace of God. The will needs a certain fear to help it properly function. Peter knew this, so he

advised his readers, "conduct yourselves with fear through-out the time of your exile" (1 Pet. 1:17). There is a legiti-mate fear that nurtures the Christian in a caution against failure. When he was a pastor in New York, Dr. John H. Jowett, the noted English preacher, preacher a sermon to his congregation on "Awe and Trust." His text was Psalm 4:4-5, akin in meaning to the verse from Peter mentioned above. Dr. Jowett deemed it wise to introduce the wording of his subject, so he explained: "This seems to be a little remote from the phraseology of modern religious life. Our vocabulary is of a different type and order. Words like awe, fear, trembling, appear to be almost obsolete. Our speech finds its emphasis in such words as happiness, joy, peace, comfort. The Psalmist throws us back to quite a different plane."

And so does our word "fear." Every Christian needs this legitimate fear that nurtures us for cautious liv-ing. Caution is needed because life is a real and important involvement. Caution is needed because God is not only Father; he is also Judge. It is possible to fail: mismanaged stress can lead to presumption, pride, carelessness, selfish-ness, worldliness, sin. This gift of fear forbids any foolish-ness and goads us against failure. Linked with a ready love for God, this fear reduces the margin for failure by keep-ing us mindful toward sobriety, piety, obedience, and gratitude.

As a gift of grace, this fear does not paralzye our efforts, it rather works to prepare us. Something Arthur Rubinstein said once will illustrate what I mean here. That versatile pianist has confessed that he is still troubled with some bit of nervousness before he plays or records, despite the fact that he has been appearing before the public as a professional artist for many decades. But Rubinstein divides the nervous states into two types. "There are two kinds of shakes. One kind is necessary to get you into the blessed state of nervous preparation. You can't become inspired without it. Once on stage I am completely relieved." The other he describes as "the paralyzing kind. If you have that, the only advice I can give is don't play in public." The fear that blesses our intent will is the kind that prepares us. It prepares us to appraise matters in seriousness and then follow what appears to be the appointed way. Such fear has to do with proper regard and responsibility before God.

This given fear can best be described as a creative caution. It is a certain concern, a saving solicitation, a dependable dread. It is a guard against any indifference or decay. It is what keeps us mindful to remain surrendered, to remember that we are dealing with *God*. This fear is a kind of unsettled intensity that is stilled only by the approval of God. Billy Sunday used to illustrate the point of Christian carefulness by telling what he had heard about the dove. "I have been told," Sunday said, "that a dove has been known to tremble when a single feather from a vulture's wing has been held in front of it." So does the cautious Christian, concerned to be in the right, tremble at even suggestions of failure on the part of a seducing Satan. This fear sensitizes the will in alertness. It is an aid against possible dishonor and ultimate damnation. This fear keeps our sense of "oughtness" centered for use. It helps our will to question all suggested possibilities of experience and test them critically against the measure of the known Word of God, as Jesus did.

THE CHRISTIAN STANCE

Peter wrote by divine prompting. We do need such a fear. And God gives it. He gives it to stir us toward the proper use of our lives in his sight. Augustine once described this fear as a piercing needle that holds the thread binding us to God.

The Privilege of Prayer

3. The will is further strengthened by the privilege of life-girding *prayer*. This "elemental function" is a divine gift set in every soul. But it must be exercised to be properly valued.

When Teresa of Avila, in her early forties, was still anxious about Christian perfection and how to attain it, she entered a prayer room at the convent to pray about it in utter seriousness. She beheld an oft-seen statue of the crucified Savior; the very sight of it so stirred her sense of emptiness and erring that she fell weeping before the statue. She vowed on her knees that she would not rise from that place until Christ had given grace sufficient to fix her forever against offending him. Her intense desire met with favor—as indeed all true prayer does. Teresa afterward realized the centered progress of soul she had sought for many years. She had poured her life into her prayer, and Christ had put his life into her as answer. The privilege of prayer is the utterly personal quality of the encounter, together with its life-girding effects.

Jesus is known to have stressed prayer as a means for girding the will. One instance is found in Mark 14:38, "Watch and pray that you may not enter into temptation; the spirit indeed is willing, but the flesh is weak." The words were not uttered, mind you, as a human excuse for failure. They were spoken with direct concern for a steadied will in a drastic encounter about to face those who heard him. Jesus understood situationed human nature, thus he advised about how to handle its limitations through enabling prayer to God. Prayer helps willingness, girding it with strength against undeniable feelings and near-unbelievable events.

There are problems peculiar to Christian experience. There are crises common to the Christian commitment. There are real dangers that test our stand. Jesus advised about alertness to hazards and prayerful action. His words still are: "Watch and pray." The watching alerts us to the conditions of crisis, while prayer grants courage for facing them; watching helps us to define what we see, while prayer grants needed defense against what we see; watching brings into play that necessary fear, while prayer releases that certain faith; we watch against hazards, and pray in hope to handle the hazards. As Samuel Johnson put it,

Father, in Thy mysterious Presence kneeling,
Fain would our souls feel all Thy kindling love;
For we are weak, and need some deep revealing
Of trust and strength and calmness from above.

Watching keeps our will alerted. Prayer guarantees that our will is aided.

This instruction from Jesus grants at least one clue about his personal strength during times of stress. This counsel to watch and pray also helps us to better understand that section of the model prayer he gave to his disciples which reads, "And lead us not into temptation, But deliver us from evil" (Matt. 6:13). The petition is twofold: Jesus tells us to pray in order to be spared, if possible; and to be granted safety in the midst of evil when we are not spared having to face it. That section of the prayer is plainly a petition of the soul for safety against possible sin when one is under stress. It is an intended line for the steadying of one's life against evil.

Deliverance from evil can mean that God will delay or even change some feared possibility for us. It can also mean that God will control us—by our prayerful consent —if the evil must be met. Prayer grants us a given strength through which to grapple and win, as when Jesus was "led up by the Spirit into the wilderness to be tempted by the devil" (Matt. 4:1). We are not always spared stress, even when we pray to be so spared; but through prayer we are granted safety. Appointed prayer strengthens the inward stance to properly handle whatever life brings us.

A collection of contemporary art was being shown at Atlanta University's Trevor Arnett Library. I was particularly stirred as I studied Benjamin Britt's provocative oil painting captioned "Yield Not!" The painting suggests the pathos felt in the experience of being tempted.

A man is shown squatting, dressed in a loose, rough garb. His head is bent between his knees and his eyes are being shielded by a protecting arm from the attractive glitter of an object lying on the ground before him. The other arm is stretched out stiffly against the object itself. The gesture is one of restraint. It is a scene of protest. It is part of a painful strategy of refusal.

The object of the refusal is a small, round, colorful substance, agate-like in its appearance. It is a thing of form, space, appealing color, and evident beauty. There it lies before the garbed man (monk?). It lies there waiting. It is a suggestive, appealing thing, something ready and available.

Therefore does he shield his eyes: that man knows the appeal of that object. He desires inner constancy—thus his outstretched hand against it. It is a provocative picture of grand refusal. He is *touched* by the experience, but he still refuses to be tripped by it. He shields his eyes to refuse the object his full attention. The emotional pull of the experience is readily sensed. That garbed figure knows what he faces, so he has set himself against failure. He has set his mind and soul not to yield. The set of his will was that man's choice and decision. The strengthening of his will demands divine gifts.

The only stance that is sure in life is that stance of a sanctified will made bold by faith, made cautious by fear, and girded by the intimacy of prayer. Blessed by such a set of sure aids, the Christian can maintain his stance, ready for God, ready for life, firmly set to "follow in his steps" (1 Pet. 2:21).

4: Stress and Sanctity

Socrates, the Grecian sage, has been quoted as saying, "The unexamined life is not worth living." We have been examining our lives. The examination has been against a background of facts from science and passages from Scripture. Extended concern has been devoted to a discussion of the common experience of temptation. We have seen ourselves engaged in an environment both moral and material, and we have charted some of our basic reactions to the environment. We have discussed the importance of a will set to do the will of God and how our intent is invested with strength through certain divine aids. We now pass on to examine our involvement with life *in terms of its meaning* for our lives. We seek to acquaint ourselves with how our living can be made to contribute to our life, how conditions can be meaningfully managed to bless our character. Thus the heading, "Stress and Sanctity."

As used here, "stress" means that which seems to oppose our working plan, making it difficult for us to achieve our end with ease; that which puts us under felt strain, tension, making us go beyond our known strength in handling some problem *and ourselves*.

"Sanctity," as used here, means simply: what results from being devoted to the will of God—from responding to his inward work and known Word, sharing progressively in his character. Sanctity is that quality of life produced when man is obedient and open to God. It is that wholeness of life made possible as we "share [in] his holiness" (Heb. 12:10).

Every true Christian knows sanctity to some degree of

experience. He knows it by virtue of his relationship with God and Christ. It is the teaching of the New Testament that sanctity is a gift of being in right relationship with God, that the separation of the self from willful sin sets a man within the will of God—and the will of God within him. This very relationship of claim and experience prompted the New Testament writers to label every Christian as a "saint." Sanctity is the result of God at work in the soul through his presence and grace, a saint being one in whom that work, grace, and presence are realized.

The very mention of the words "saint" and "holy" in our time evokes in so many minds the figured image of some monk in isolation, or some especially gifted person bent upon fasting and enmeshed in spiritual ecstasies or ascetic excesses. But sainthood does not necessarily issue from seclusion, deep sorrow over sins of the past, nor ascetic practices per se. Sanctity is the gift of the presence of God in the soul; it is the result of his work in the life. A saint is one who lives in steady correspondence with Jesus Christ through faith and devotion; one who is open to the further working of God to shape him to the full character of Jesus as "the Beloved" (Eph. 1:6). The saint is a God-claimed person whose life shows that claim.

Sanctity, then, is given. But it can grow. It can increase. It can deepen. It can mature. We have agreed earlier that our lives are essentially unfinished, that we all have within ourselves that which seeks to be fulfilled. For the Christian, sanctification is the ordained province within which the shaping and fulfillment are sought—and directed. The experience of stress plays an important role in that whole process.

70

STRESS AND SANCTITY

Stress Brings Exercise

1. Stress is important to sanctity because *it prompts the exercise of the soul.* There is no moral growth apart from moral struggle. There can be no increase of spiritual strength apart from spiritual pain. Strength in godliness is dependent upon our handling of stress.

We are augmented in the midst of struggle. In some unique manner pain serves personality and blesses our selfhood. Stress makes us feel separate, incomplete, threatened, and at a loss. The very struggle with these feelings must be from within a structured faith. We struggle with an object and a goal in mind; we can fight with a decided direction for our lives in view. We fight in given freedom to shift our interest or steadily pursue our chosen end. When we hold this will to remain godly, we have progress, but it is a progress in pain. What we *feel* in the struggle is not the tragic factor; but what we *will* during the struggle becomes the factor for triumph. By means of that will, we wrest from the struggle strength for ourselves. This is a condition for the whole of our lives and not just to be applied to the realm of the spiritual. Stress is a basic ingredient of life. This fact need not disrupt us. It should rather alert us to one means by which God has planned our progress. The Christian can make his struggles serve his soul.

Some years ago Dr. W. Melville Arnott, then professor of medicine at the University of Birmingham, in England, presented a paper on work to the Royal Society of Medicine. He stated that work, even hard work, is good for a person, while rest, on the other hand, may be quite damaging in the long run. He was careful to point out that work got a bad name when exploitation of workers was so evident during the last century. But he insisted that work is not basically unhealthy, even as much as a forty-hour workweek in a modern factory or shop setting. He stated that none of the known effects of normal work can harm healthy tissues; on the contrary, they rather serve to develop and extend the range of the abilities of our physiological mechanism. Rest, on the other hand, can be damaging. Blood circulation is affected by it; muscles lose their needed tone; appetite slackens; constipation is also a threatening factor. (It is only at acute stages of illness that bed rest even is advised.)

Dr. Arnott's report has implications for the spiritual life as well. Just as the body is blessed and served by the stress and strain which exercise it, so is the soul blessed and served by comparable stress and strain on its level. The experience of stress has its meaning. The circumstances of our days actually tend to complement our days, when we answer those circumstances with proper inward attitudes and actions. When we exercise our power to do what we have willed under God, the passionate action that must follow strengthens Christian character.

Strain Sets Patterns

2. Stress is important to sanctity again because *it permits the pattern of godliness to become more deeply ingrained*. It has been mentioned earlier that a new form and dimension of life is made available to us in Christ. That new form shapes itself progressively within us during our struggles. This is important both ethically and practically. Having made the decision to live with and for God, the mind finds itself renewed whenever that decision is tested by life and evil. It is not merely a matter of obeying divine

directions handed down; it is a matter of gaining insight into the reality of divine presence while under stress. It is a known fact that temptation, for instance, is all the more terrible when one does not yield; the full force of the experience is felt because one wills to stand despite having to go through the complete cycle of the test. The man who yields never realizes the depth of grace the successful soul plumbs in his will to stand.

The man who continues his stand with God learns increasingly how much God stands with him. His intent is deepened and so is his sense of guidance, help, and worth. The man who suffers, with his heart set on God, sees God in the struggle. This means that while the roots of his loyalty are being checked under trial, the character of his life is being strengthened by his increased vision. Martin Luther might well have been speaking about this when he wrote, "I did not learn my divinity [theology] at once, but I was constrained by my temptations to search deeper and deeper." It is true: our knowledge of God is dependent upon our experiences of stress.

Stress Shows Us Up

3. An increasing knowledge of self is also important for our Christian maturity. *Stress helps to show us ourselves.* Douglas V. Steere tells of an experience that helps us to better grasp the point of this statement. He was with his wife, visiting in Holland. They were walking one Sunday afternoon along a street where a noted church stood. They noticed, while passing, the high flight of stone steps, about thirty-five or forty in all, leading up to the church door from the street below. A child of about three years of age had climbed those steps and was standing at the top.

THE SOUL UNDER SIEGE

He was full of glee over his accomplishment and was calling back down in happiness to his watching parents. Steere and his wife continued to watch. They soon saw that the child sensed his problem: how to get back down those steps to his parents!

The child called for his father to come up and get him. The father stood still and rather beckoned for the child to come down alone. The little adventurer, full of fear, began to shout defiantly; he stamped his feet and protested. The father still did not move forth to get him. The child soon tired of himself. He cautiously (and cryingly) put one foot on the top step, followed it with the other foot just below, and slowly—so slowly at first—descended the steps in obedience. All adults below were anxious for him: a fall could have been damaging with serious lacerations or dislocation of bones. A fall could have been fatal! When he at last reached the bottom the child rushed at full speed into the arms of his waiting father, who hugged him warmly and then walked on with the family now at ease.

The descent of that child alone had been costly. But the lesson was quite important for his self-understanding and growth. The father had risked that lesson in love.

Like that child, we, too, are sometimes under pressure and strain in our life under love. But our learning demands such stress. The learning has to do with the courage to risk ourselves to the wisdom of God. We must learn how to handle life by *facing it;* God so wills that we be tutored in necessary risks. We learn to trust his love and not our illegitimate fears. God knows the cost of our risks. There is not only the cost we feel, there is cost to himself. But God has refused to keep us separated from necessary affairs of risk and ventures that can discipline our spirits.

STRESS AND SANCTITY

Stress makes us take a good look at ourselves. As our strength of purpose is put to the test, the needy areas of our lives are uncovered. We become conscious of weak spots within ourselves. In seeing ourselves we sense our need. But it is at this precise point of felt need that the love of God is also sensed. Touching the deepest areas within us, awakening all there is to be found, stress shows us just where more conditioning is needed. *Stress makes us aware that we are still in process.* Humiliation can result. But so can hope. Humiliation can result because the conflict so pressures the self, and because, as Wayne E. Oates has explained, "The conflictual character of the course of Christian development is not a smoothly contoured ascent from one stage to another. Nor is it ever completed and finished." Hope, however, can hold us steady in faith since we know that the Incarnation shows us a life of purpose. Linked with Christ, we, too, shall know the complete and satisfactory end of the process. We hope because "God is for us" (Rom. 8:31). We hope because the stress will have an approved issue under God. As Bernard Ramm comments, "God has made our cause his cause." The Christian is not at the hands of fate while he struggles. He is in the hands of his Father. With this understanding of himself, the Christian can afford to face life and not fear it.

4. With this understanding of himself, it should also be clear to the Christian that *God never ordains failure for any man nor must he be blamed when failure occurs.* According to James 1:2f, the testing time must be viewed as prelude to blessing. "Count it all joy, my brethren, when

you meet various trials, for you know that the testing of your faith produces steadfastness. And let steadfastness have its full effect, that you may be perfect and complete, lacking in nothing." But some regard the testing not as blessing but as a blight. James 1:13-14 speaks on this point. "Let no one say when he is tempted, 'I am tempted by God'; for God cannot be tempted with evil and he himself tempts no one; but each person is tempted when he is lured and enticed by his own desire." James only reminds us here that stress *can* end in sin when the self is not properly set to handle it. Stress can degrade us, but that is not the will of God for us. God is concerned about our development, conditioning, steadfastness, character. God never sets a trap for Christians.

I am reminded at this point of a conversation I had with a young man on a beach in Jamaica some years ago. He had used an entire afternoon to flirt with passion; prolonged embracing of his girl friend made this quite open and evident. When I was ready to leave the beach I paused long enough to advise him against his improper conduct. I was quite pointed in my remarks about self-control. The young girl hung her head in shame. The young man also dropped his head as I spoke. But after admitting his wrong he raised his head and asked, in a spirit of defiance prompted by the will to "be free": "Why did God make us like this?" I answered both his statement and his state. God has shaped us with needs, desires, and many possibilities within our reach. He did not start us off at a handicap but rather placed us under trust.

The Christian must also keep this in mind. He is under trust. He has met God's trust with faith in God's provisions for his life. He knows reconciliation. He has renewal. He has identity in Christ. He is not *what he was before*. But he is not fully what he was designed to be. The stance he takes in life will help him to grow and mature in Christ, provided it is matched by an understood relationship of trust in God's way with man. God does not ordain failure but our fulfillment. No human power was set to corrupt us but to complement us.

5. Again, stress blesses sanctity in that *it keeps us sensitively dependent upon the example and enablement of Jesus*. Watching Jesus as supreme example, "The self both lays hold of and is laid hold of by the purpose of God in Christ." The writer to the Hebrews had this in mind when he counseled them, in the midst of their stress-ridden days, to keep "looking to Jesus the pioneer and perfecter of our faith . . ." (12:2). Jesus stands before our faith as a tested but triumphant Son. He is one able "to sympathize with our weaknesses, but one who in every respect has been tempted as we are, yet without sinning" (Heb. 4:15). His situations were real and exacting like our own. The range of his tests was like those we know, and he was faced with the possible directions into which the desires of men erringly venture: wrath, envy, lust, gluttony, covetousness, sloth, and pride. But Jesus had taken his stance before God and before life. He therefore "committed no sin; no guile was found on his lips" (1 Pet. 2:22).

As one who has been tested, Jesus stands before us as one who *knows*. His steadfastness under siege sobers our self-concern and reminds us of our necessary purpose under God. Character must be shaped in a God-approved way. Even Jesus "learned obedience through what he suffered" (Heb. 5:8). It is not inevitable that a man deviate when under stress. He can develop. Jesus stands before us as supreme proof. This reassures the soul under siege.

The influence of tested character is especially relevant for us. We see in the one who has succeeded what we can be and do. Jesus stands before us as our Man of measure. He shows us in himself the rewards and worthiness of a resolute stand in life. It is not to be wondered that in Hebrews 2:13 we read these words on the lips of Jesus, "I will put my trust in him." Jesus, too, had to give himself over for safekeeping to God. God would make him emerge in triumph.

Sanctity is deepened as we live without panic, on the one hand, and without pride, on the other. Watching Jesus helps us in both instances. He faced felt stress with resolution, kept his aspiration high, and sought God for guidance. Watching all this in the life of Jesus, we remain sensitive to our need to so respond. We thereby continue our commitment and further condition our sanctity.

Dr. Robert J. McCracken tells in one of his sermons about a certain shopkeeper in Brighton, England, who was a member of the church pastored by the great preacher Frederick William Robertson. The man's esteem for his pastor was so great that he kept a portrait of him in a little room at the back of his shop. During the course of a day, whenever he was tempted to err in business matters, the shopkeeper would go back to that room and pause before his pastor's picture: the looking served to steady him against some tempting suggestion. He wanted to be true, for he knew someone who trusted him, someone whose trust meant so much. That man's pastor helped him with his conduct. The influence of Jesus can be likened to that, but with a deeper thrust.

STRESS AND SANCTITY

There is a passage in *The Robe,* by Lloyd Douglas, that also treats this matter of his influence when we are under stress. Douglas has Justus, now converted, say to Marcellus about Jesus, "Sometimes I feel aware of him as if he were close by. It keeps you honest." He added, "It is a great satisfaction to have someone standing by—to keep you at your best." The will does need a stimulus. The Christian finds this all in Jesus. He looks both *at* Jesus and *to* him. He looks at him as supreme example; he looks to him as enabler. As the words of Marcellus remind us, Jesus watches even as we watch. He is concerned about our state. Linked with us in a solidarity that saves us, he watches us in order to prompt, encourage, caution, correct, and cheer. It is not mere sentimentality to regard Jesus in this way. The picture in Hebrews 12:1-2 declares that Jesus is so linked with us, watching our way with understanding, sympathy, empathy, and regard. Jesus watches us and speaks to us, advising and assuring. It *is* a great satisfaction to have him standing by during our time of stress. In his presence we realize more fully the height and depth and breadth and length of the goodness of God toward us. In his presence we deepen and guard our granted sanctity.

6. There is still another way in which stress holds meaning for our lives: *when we properly handle stress, God uses the victory as reason to further bless our lives.* James 1:12 holds this promise. "Blessed is the man who endures trial, for when he has stood the test he will receive the crown of life which God has promised to those who love him." Steadfastness under stress is proof of our love for God. God, in turn, rewards our stand. In fact, God con-

gratulates us. The Greek word James used for "blessed" is a loaded term. It was an expression of congratulation when someone was being honored for some noble deed or accomplishment. Private letters from the first century show this use. The Jewish heritage of James is also in his use of the term; he knew through the Old Testament teachings that God rewards men for faithfulness.

Works are important when done in the spirit of gratitude and with an understanding of grace. The thought is heartening when we are under stress. God crowns the Christian who lives up to the name. He gives him "life," that vital force that grants fullness to our days and glory to our future. The reference is not merely eschatological, as with the same phrase in Rev. 2:10, "Be faithful unto death, and I will give you the crown of life"; it involves the Christian's present. God grants the man who stands the honor of having stood. He congratulates that man's deed as an act of love and draws near to him, honoring his life by His crowning presence. God makes such a man aware of the change and growth he has gained. This grants a joy especially one's own. This is highly important and meaningful for selfhood. It is this that stands behind the Christian's joy. The man who lasts through the stress, resolved to honor God while in it, is the man who finds himself happy. He realizes that he has been crowned with joy. So Martin Luther wrote, "It is impossible for one who hopes in God not to rejoice." The "crowned" Christian readily agrees.

Life does have its hard spots, its places of peril. Life can often seem like a giant system of trial. The Christian need not view life as accidental—"lacking in design." He holds to faith that stress and siege are essential, that they serve the interests of God in man, that they can be handled with resolve and the grace of God. There is a law in life that development is dependent upon struggle: we must conquer that which in the struggle can yield to us its strength. We can achieve only as we act, investing ourselves in faith, hope, and love. So sanctity comes. So sanctity grows. So sanctity becomes a seen challenge.

The closing pages of Bunyan's *Pilgrim's Progress* show many pilgrims crossing over the River Jordan. The faithful take time to speak encouraging words to those being left behind. A line from Mr. Standfast rises from those pages like a high mountain peak: "I have loved to hear my Lord spoken of, and wherever I have seen the print of his shoe in the earth, there I have coveted to set my foot too."

Our Lord walked that dangerous road called *stress*. And there were redemptive results!

5: Prayer and Sanctity

"Discover what service a thing renders," writes James McKechnie, "and you have discovered why it finds a place in the universe." Prayer will never lose its place—its services are too central for the life and lot of man. Prayer girds our lives. It is the most important undertaking possible for us because it provides essential communion with God. Prayer is no secret real or isolated fact. It is an open, vital, centered experience. Prayer is depth living with God, the dialogue in which selfhood is honored, sustained, renewed, and shared. The relation of prayer to Christian sanctity, then, is indispensable.

Prayer As Attentiveness

Prayer blesses sanctity because it is the most vital way of being attentive to God. It is the focus of the self upon the spiritual order of life. It is our open attention to an attentive God. Prayer is the conscious outgoing of the self to meet with God in willed encounter. That attentive act, however brief or lengthy contributes vitally to a given sanctity. That attentive act is important to the attitude we hold toward living.

As the way of being attentive to God, the act of prayer therefore demands a centered attention. Broken or wandering attention has spoiled many occasions when prayer could have been an experience of depth. Broken or wandering attention in prayer invariably has its sad effects in our lives. He who does not *set* himself to truly pray finds that he is not really set for a life in honor of God.

82

PRAYER AND SANCTITY

It must be noted that our age has shown a considerable decline in the ability to remain attentive for considerable periods of time. This is an indication of a crucial problem in the modern use of the mind. Even the more excellent reading matter—the "Great Books" for instance—greatly hailed and read during earlier decades by the educated, is being neglected. It is true that *such* reading *is* demanding. Journalistic agencies have been quick to sense the modern laziness of mind and have produced shorter and simplified versions of what can be read. The packaged reading of our day has been produced in remarkably brief accounts. Few demands are made today upon readers of the "popular" literature; it is popular because it is less demanding. Added to this fact is another—things of considered importance for the public are readily processed now for viewing. Consequently, an unending stream of pictorial magazines is available at every corner store. The demand for materials that can be quickly scanned does recognize the fact that our times move at faster pace and are quite filled with things to do; but it is still to be lamented that only a scattered minority seeks valuable and solid prose or is discontent with mere capsule-knowledge. So everything is carefully measured, reduced to capsule form, and calculated not to fatigue or lay much demand upon eye or mind.

Clifton Fadiman writes, "In general, a successful, technically admirable attempt is made to *attract* the attention without actually engaging it." Discipline, for reading or for the deeper issue of living itself, is a passing demand. Modernity in the physical and commercial aspects of life has taken its toll upon the men of our times. Few perceive the profound; their interest is elsewhere or their time is too short. Our very age moves without depth or vision, too hurried to sense the glory that the presence of the holy reveals. The Christian must help bring a return to God's order—an order that demands his disclosed pattern and our disciplined will. The Christian can hope to gain the attention of the world when he remains attentive to God himself by both prayerful attitude *and* the *attentive action of prayer*.

Prayer demands a mind attentive to God. In another book of mine I sought to trace out some of the conflicts that can beset the person at prayer: distractions, dryness, delays, denials, doubts. The person intent to pray must sometimes struggle his way to attention.

John Donne wrote of his struggle to be attentive to God during the prayer time. His experience will be seen at once to run true to what so many, many others can well confess about themselves.

> But when we consider with a religious seriousness the manifold weaknesses of the strongest devotions in time of Prayer, it is a sad consideration. I throw my selfe downe in my chamber, and I call in, and invite God, and his Angels thither, and when they are there, I neglect God and his Angels, for the noise of a Flie, for the Ratling of a Coach, for the whining of a doore; I talke on, in the same posture of praying; Eyes lifted up; knees bowed downe; as though I prayed to God, and, if God, or his Angels aske me, when I thought last of God in that prayer, I cannot tell: Sometimes I finde that I had forgot what I was about, but when I began to forget it, I cannot tell. A memory of yesterdays pleasures, a feare of tomorrows dangers, a straw under my knee, a noise in mine eare, a light in mine eye, an any thing, a nothing, a fancy, a Chimera in my braine, troubles me in my prayer.

The temptation at such a time is to speak hurriedly to God or to cease speaking to him altogether for a time. There is a lack of comfort and centeredness that bids us rise and run. The solution to this problem is not always to be sought in delaying the time of prayer. The answer is to be found in a deep intent to truly pray. Communion-mindedness for the time of prayer follows from a mind attentive to God in other aspects of life. Attention in prayer is sustained through the daily practice of his presence. Sanctity deepens when our prayer is from the heart.

How long must the prayer time be? Joseph Parker has given prompt answer, saying, "No prayer is long that is prayed with the heart: as long as the heart can talk the prayer is very brief—let that be the measure and standard of our long and much praying. Do not measure your prayers by minutes, but by necessities. He added, "A day's long talk, a night's long communion, will be but too short, if you see the King as it were face to face."

Prayer As Transaction

Prayer blesses sanctity because it permits and yields an essential transaction with God. Prayer proceeds best when there is the conviction that the "meeting" with God will indeed *happen.* When such anticipation is present, attention can be more readily centered, and stirrings within the self more readily settled. Anticipation alerts the soul to expect something transcendent and transforming. The moment with God *is* transcendent. We learn far more than we can explain, and we experience far more than we can readily understand. So much of the encounter never yields to our attempts to frame it into exact, precise statements. There will always be some aspects of the experience of prayer that will defy final description. This is so because prayer is an essential *transaction* with God; there is definite action across the gulf that separates Holiness from humanity. The life is distinctly touched and the mind is left with a task. When there is true prayer, the soul does see "the King as it were face to face." That is the anticipation that stirs to prayer. Augustine wrote about his reaction to this need. "I draw back in terror in so far as I am different from Him; yet I am on fire with longing in the degree of my likeness to Him." Holiness settles our humanity when we pray. The encounter is creative for the self.

The encounter with God is also creative beyond the self. Prayer grants a service to all the levels of our lives. It is an appointed means for creation as well as control. The given intimacy with God can grant us help on any needed level—moral, material, and miraculous. God fixes few limits for those who fix themselves to truly pray.

Bringing with us a strict sense of attention and an intense anticipation, our experience of prayer can guide us through the maze of critical human life. Prayer can help us to sense connections between God and ourselves; to see him at work in our life and in our world. Prayer can grant us insights. Prayer can strangely but surely lead us to granted needs, answered petitions, and guarded sanctity. Prayer is the experience of meeting with God in the stream of one's own time and seeing into eternity. When we pray, we punctuate time to reach for what is eternal. The life of God and man intersect at prayer. As Thomas S. Eliot put it in *The Dry Savages,*

> *To apprehend*
> *The point of intersection of the timeless*
> *With time is an occupation for the saint.*

The saint enjoys his work. He lives by that sensed intersection. He lives by those moments of eternal meaning. He rejoices in the mystic moment when truth is seen in focus and an experience becomes finally full. The saints have no other "secret" than this—they learned to pray. They had essential transactions with God. Such praying kept them willing partners in prayer-speech with God. Such prayer also kept them probing their lives for strict order and attentiveness to the will of God. Such prayer kept them prodded toward sanctity in full dimension.

Prayer blesses sanctity because it provides a point for the abandonment of self to God. During prayer the Christian can rehearse his ground for confidence to live. He can take a fresh, courageous stand upon the realities of grace. He can examine his experience and his responses. He can permit God to deal with him at those depths of personality that need and require God's helpful, readying touch.

The encounter with God in prayer helps to break fresh ground in a man's life. As heart touches heart, as truth and thought meet, there is an exacting offer and demand. Self-life must yield for the sharing of love. Classifications break down, but closeness is evident and sure. The mind stands startled, but the life is now steadied. It is a self-emptying that is both demanded and felt. God fills those places that we held before in strict privacy—places we did not know were even there before! We must trust ourselves to the import of the moment of truth. What we have been living is made to erupt in our view; all individualism and private pretensions are put under due judgment. In our yielding to God's offer and demands, he grants us something that will be an eternal joy to keep. That something is realized kinship—sanctity. And this is the life we increasingly learn to prize.

THE SOUL UNDER SIEGE

God and Man

It was said in an earlier chapter that it takes God to explain man. It also takes God to fulfill him. This is not only the biblical view; it is the foundation fact beneath the concerns of religions throughout the ages. Whatever the varieties of religious experience—and they are many, the demand is structured in our being for relatedness to God, to Another, to God who determines and guarantees and fulfills us according to his eternal purpose. Where there is the notion of no God, or a sense that he is absent, man tends to lose his identity. The self needs the context of thought about God and the active concerns of God operating in its interest. Man cannot live by logic but by life, by that kind of life that is always open, promising, quick, impressive, resting in the love of God. Biblical religion deals always and increasingly with the relations between God and the self, with that dynamic area of life described by Martin Buber as "the realm of 'between.' " The love-bond between God and man *is* vital religion. We realize that love-bond when prayer is at its best.

Prayer opens us consciously and regularly to our Source. It keeps us "religious" in the truest sense of the word. Life did not start in us, it only flows there, and it is within that we realize life. When we take this seriously, we will be concerned to have a religious experience that is intensive without being abnormal. The human psyche has a genuine activity of a spiritual nature. If there is anything the psychologists have made plain to us it is that the spiritual order of life has its claims, its terms, its sanctions and incentives. And if there is anything that the Bible

88

PRAYER AND SANCTITY

seeks to make clear it is that a human experience at its best demands the recognition of and response to the Holy. An adequate sense of life depends upon our dependence upon the Holy. God is accessible to us; we are accountable for our response—or lack of response—to God. The life of man is of wide content but the total content falls, by divine right, under the claim of God. Our life involves nature, but a nature in which God shares. Our life is personal, but the context of the personal is conditioned as being "in the image of God." Our life is essentially and necessarily religious, for both sense and Spirit meet within us. We are conditioned for response. The man who truly prays, lives out his response.

The response of which I speak is not to be restricted, however. Religious experience at its best exacts of us an inward structuring of concern to handle all living, all reality, religiously. It is handling of all partials by one unique, God-required and God-given particular—*love toward God*. Jesus laid his finger of stress on this point when he restated what Moses gave as *the* chief commandment: "And you shall love the Lord your God with all your heart, and with all your soul, and with all your mind, and with all your strength" (Mark 12:30; see also Deut. 6:5). I need not remind you that although several aspects of the human self are being distinguished in that saying it is to show that the whole self must respond lovingly toward God. Every faculty and all creaturely powers are involved—consciousness, constitution, and concern. Loving response to God, free from all reticence and restraint, is a prime essential for what we usually term "spirituality."

THE SOUL UNDER SIEGE

True Spirituality

This spirituality should be understood to mean our relationship with the ordinary world under the guidance of values anchored in our experience with God's love. Spirituality has to do with the total life of man under God; man living in the world by God's terms; man living with openness toward God, drawing strength from what happens between them. Spirituality is humanity wedded to holiness. It is not a denial of the world, but a proper handling of the world.

I am recalling here what Paul sought to point out when he wrote that Christians must "deal with the world as though they had no dealings with it" (1 Cor. 7:31a)— use its offerings as things on loan, things we will not and cannot permanently possess. Spirituality is the *initiation* of the will and self to live by love to God. Our love to God is not at first of finished character; it fashions us even as it is being fashioned through God's love toward us. Spirituality is still more: it is *enthusiastic follow-through* of the self after the initiation. It is being "led by the Spirit," as Paul put it in Galatians 5:18. It is holding to what has been introduced to us in Christ. It is being held, willingly, within the expressed desires of God. Spirituality is the state of willing no interruption between the self and God. It is to appreciate all that is necessary to cultivate that love-bond, and to resist all that stands opposed to it. Spirituality, then, is both a contingent and a constraint. It is a tendency, not a finality; a principal, not a religion; a way, not a goal. The true goal is uninterrupted love-life with God.

This emphasis upon loving God and abandoning oneself to him is reminiscent of overt mysticism. The informed

PRAYER AND SANCTITY

Christian knows that there is no need to speak with restraint on this matter, for he is conscious of the accessibility of God. He knows that God is found by "pledging a self," as Martin Buber put it, responsibly to God. The pledge is matched by God in breaking through complicated personal walls, exposing unworthy formations of the self, and granting the self its moment of release in the realized love of God. This is essential religious experience. It is a fact sanctioned by the greatest declarations in the New Testament and illustrated in the encounters of men with the Christ of God. Consider these declarations: "Come to me, all who labor and are heavy laden, and I will give you rest. Take my yoke upon you, and learn from me; for I am gentle and lowly in heart, and you will find rest for your souls" (Matt. 11:28-29); "I came that they may have life, and have it abundantly" (John 10:10*b*).

As for the encounters, the literature is abundant, both in the pages of the Bible and elsewhere. Would not the many witnesses each confess that he became free and established through the shared "secret"? His heart questioned and God replied to it in truth. The monologue of self-life became the dialogue of self-with-God-in-love. The dynamic of the event is a kind of "secret," known, as indeed it must be, only by the longing heart and the pledged self. The "secret"?—God in Christ, and "Christ in you, the hope of glory" (Col. 1:27). Paul spent his ministry years proclaiming "the riches of the glory of this mystery." His word for *mystery* means a deed of God too profound for human reason, and known only as revealed by God. Christian faith involves a mysticism. In fact, Christian experience demands one. Prayer to God is always a mystic's action—and a practical human need.

THE SOUL UNDER SIEGE

God has structured within us the need to abandon ourselves to him.

Prayer and Power

The abandonment of self to God through prayer enables us to stand up better under the stress of life. It prepares us to gain and hold successes in life. It also prepares us to properly handle ourselves when some life ventures do not bless our efforts as we had wanted. While he was a student at Julliard, Van Cliburn was recommended by the school to enter the Michaels Award Competition in Chicago. The winner of first prize would receive one thousand dollars plus numerous concert engagements with major symphony orchestras in the nation. Cliburn got through the preliminary hearings in which two to three hundred instrumentalists took part. He then went on as one of the surviving twenty-five into the semifinals. Mme. Lhevinne had been coaching Cliburn for his role. Knowing that he prays about every major action, she said to him one day, "I suppose you're praying you'll win in Chicago?" Young Cliburn answered with studied words, "No, I'm praying God to give me the strength to bear it if I don't come through."

Some years ago Dr. Otto Weininger of the University of Toronto reported on the importance of T.L.C. (tender loving care) to babies. The report was made at a meeting of the American Association for the Advancement of Science. The point of the studies was that babies who are given "tender loving care" will be better able to stand stresses and less likely to develop troubles in blood, heart, or stomach as they grow up than those babies who do not receive such treatment. Extensive studies dealing with a daily "gentling" of baby rats seemed to show this.

PRAYER AND SANCTITY

According to the *Science News Letter* in which the report appeared,

> The gentling consisted of holding the rat nestled in the scientist's hand close to his chest and stroking its back from the head to base of the tail.
>
> These gentled rats gained more weight, their bones grew more and they were less fearful in a strange situation. When put under severe stress as adults, including being held immobile and without food or water for 48 hours, the gentled animals showed less damage to heart, blood vessels, stomach and intestines than the nongentled ones.

That "gentling" process worked fundamental results for emotional and gladular balance. The nervous system of the "gentled" rats did not respond as excitedly to stress and alarm as did that of the non-gentled ones.

That series of studies with rats has held important implications for the inner development of growing babies. My wife Gwendolyn, a nurse, has related to me how effective tender loving care has been in situations faced by prematurely born babies, as well as children with illnesses that are prolonged.

There are tremendous implications here also for Christians solicitous about their welfare when under stress. The self-abandonment that prayer exacts on our part grants God the freedom to "gentle" us, to relate us consciously to his needed love. Prayer influences our experiences of stress because it enables us to respond to stress without undue alarm. God meets us in prayer in a way that lasts with us when we are in peril. He assures us for life through sharing his love with us. There is no substitute for *this* experience. In this way, prayer is God's means of meeting "the inner need for love," as Howard Thurman has called it.

Prayer is crucial for the self. It is the way of being attentive to God. It permits God and the self to *meet* in essential transaction. It demands that self-abandonment to God that makes us increasingly share his love. That love prepares us for our journey in life, however individual that journey must be. It is such love that casts out fear.

Prayer is crucial to sanctity. We, therefore, understand this reminder from W. E. Sangster: "There is no instance of one great in sanctity who was not great in prayer."

6: The Christian Use of Life

Dr. William Culbertson recalls the advice of Dr. J. Stuart Holden to a group of seminarians he was addressing. "Young men," he advised, "do not pray for God to use you—pray that God will make you usable." The preacher was not playing with words. His point was vital. There is a secret that guarantees the Christian use of our lives.

Our lives find and follow their Christian use only when the self is utterly dedicated to God. In a passage that is now classic, Paul called that dedication a "sacrifice" of the self. Writing to Christians at Rome, he said: "I appeal to you therefore, brethren, by the mercies of God, to present your bodies as a living sacrifice, holy and acceptable to God, which is your spiritual worship." He then continued, "Do not be conformed to this world but be transformed by the renewal of your mind, that you may prove what is the will of God, what is good and acceptable and perfect" (12:1-2).

The insistence is brief and clearly put: the Christian use of our lives is serving the will of God. It is discerning and displaying that will with strict intent. The only means to that worthy end is the sacrifice of self to God. Let us examine the insistence and its importance in detail.

The Sacrifice of Self

Paul makes his appeal against a worthy, well-known background—the realized mercies of God, the compassions we have experienced in our behalf. The term is plural because God's kindnesses to us have been abundant. They have been strikingly displayed in the steadfast love that forgave and sustains us.

Paul has used a strong word: *sacrifice*. The term reminds one essentially of a death drama. It pictures something offered in behalf of someone. It shows the utter and decisive yielding of a life in appointed order. That word *present* echoes the old Hebrew procedure of sacrifice: the priest submits the victim, offering it bodily—and in hope—to God. The term *body* represents the seat of the life being yielded; it is the visible aspect of the sacrifice.

Paul has used a strong, suggestive word, but he was careful to point out a precise meaning. He was mindful to clarify and qualify the picture in his words, knowing what such words would convey. He did mean sacrifice, but he wanted the readers to know that his appeal was toward an experience of life and not some act of real death. Observe, then, his qualifying adjective, "a *living* sacrifice." His call was not to a death, then, but rather to a dedication to God that is as decisive as death.

Nor does this sacrifice permit a substitute. The self is offered. The life remains, but it is released in dedication to a new level of use, surrendered on purpose to the will of God. The self is forever thereafter a means to divine purpose. It is then "holy"—really separated unto God. It is also "acceptable" since it meets the requirements established by God for proper use.

In using the word *sacrifice* Paul has called for a life of dedication that is as decisive and final and unchangeable as death itself.

Paul has an added word on the point. He has called the sacrifice of self a "spiritual worship." He meant that such self-giving is the most reasonable worship we can offer God. He meant that it is the most logical action expected from those who properly consider God's mercies toward them. It is only reasonable that God will use men who so give themselves. The sacrifice of self is the secret behind the Christian use of our lives.

1. The sacrifice is reasonable because we thereby return ourselves to our owner. We belong to God. It is idolatrous to take what belongs to God and transfer it to another.

2. The sacrifice of self is reasonable because we thus let God hold our lives by our voluntary consent. The resignation must be always by uncoerced loyalty. God delights in men who surrender to him in willing consent.

David Livingstone told about a very powerful chief, Sechele by name, head of the Bakwain tribe, with whom he had shared friendship and also taught to read. On one occasion, after hearing Livingstone preach to his people without full response, the chief said to Livingstone, "Do you imagine you will get these people to believe by just talking to them? I can do nothing without thrashing them. If you want them to believe, I, and my under-chiefs, will get our whips of rhinoceros' hide, and soon make them all believe."

But God does not so act. It is true that his summons always calls for a verdict, but the demand is never a thrust of tyranny. It is rather the inescapable thrust of illuminating, convicting truth. There is no coercion except that strange but sure compulsion of naked light and needed love. God always delights in willing allegiance, not forced service.

3. The sacrifice of self to God is reasonable because we thus act toward God in kind. We thereby respond to his

self-giving by our self-giving. We do because he has first done so. So God claims our lives, causing them to reflect what was seen in Jesus Christ. God blesses us to discern and display his will in able, proving fashion. Our lives can thereby stand before the world as monuments of devotion and proof of his work.

4. The sacrifice of self to God is reasonable because we are thus taken beyond ourselves—the will of God becomes the center of our experienced life. We find a distinct "set of soul" in that new context of desire. It is possible then to hold only his will as dear, willing at any time to risk our all for the sake of Christ. Because we make the supreme surrender all other "sacrificial" acts are quite easily handled.

This all means that as surrendered selves we keep ourselves available only for holy uses. We keep ourselves within interests "acceptable to God" and which alone are reasonable for us. This is the Christian way of balance in such a world. That balance guarantees that we will wield the proper influence—the "flow" from our lives into other loves we touch will remain a distinctly Christian issue. This balance delights God because our view will always involve more than the limited angles of earth. Our vision of life will extend beyond this life, because our lives are blessed from beyond this life.

Dr. George A. Buttrick tells of an experience that followed an address he gave to a group of university students. He had welcomed questions raised by his speech. Most of the questions concerned ethics. Someone said, "Right and wrong are only relative." The wise preacher admitted that, but asked, "But relative to what?" Active student minds quickly answered, "Relative to man"; "Relative to nothing"; "Relative to what's relative."

THE CHRISTIAN USE OF LIFE

With a touch of ready humor Dr. Buttrick interjected, "I never knew I had so many relatives!" Another student entered the verbal arena and charged, "It is better to be honest." The preacher reminded him that both "better" and "honest" were words of judgment and comparison, hence even they were relative to some sovereign Absolute. Another lad was now somewhat heated by all the discussion. He charged the group with foolishness, saying, "Oh, that's just playing with words." The preacher replied with skill and Christian concern: "That would be *better* than playing with *life*."

Paul's rule for the sacrifice of the self to God guards us forever against playing with our lives. Every man mishandles himself until he lets God take him beyond himself through self-giving. Small wonder, then, that the Christian differs in his approach to life and in the answers he holds regarding life itself. The Christian sees things from a higher view. He draws upon what God has said and lives by that given Word with all seriousness.

Thus the renewal of his mind. Thus his conformity to Christ. Thus his moral distance from the spirit of the age. He has placed himself where he belongs: in the hands and purpose of God.

So taken beyond ourselves we even see ourselves in a different light. This includes mind, body, and circumstances. As for the mind, we are eager to watch lest knowledge of aptitude and advantage lead to arrogance and headiness. On the other hand, we are also content knowing that conversion did not give new brains or new mental capacities as such. We accept what is given, thank God for the new context in which to use it, and value it all as a gift and a trust.

THE SOUL UNDER SIEGE

As for the body, we refuse to view it as a prison or as vile. It too is in our trust. It is reported that when Archbishop Whately lay dying, he had his chaplain read passages from the Bible to him as comfort. The chaplain read Philippians 3. He was about to end the chapter, reading those words at verse 21, "who shall change our vile body, that it may be fashioned like unto his glorious body. . . ." Whatley was weak but still alert. He asked for that verse to be read in the original, which puts it, "the body of our humiliation." Having heard that, the Archbishop relaxed, saying, "Yes, that is what St. Paul meant. Nothing that God has made is vile." The Christian can view his body as an instrument of value. The body has its proper use and its assured end—resurrection.

As for circumstances, the Christian even holds a higher view regarding them. He stands where Paul stood when he said, "We know that in everything God works for good with those who love him, who are called according to his purpose" (Rom. 8:28).

5. The giving of self to God is reasonable because such giving is the supreme proof of our religious concern. "Religious" must be understood here to mean our honest intent to be bound with God; it should mean the definite clasping of our hand and his hand. When a man so takes God's hand, giving his own in voluntary yielding, he becomes proof of his religious concern.

The whole self will know the power of that religious act. The bodily and mental powers will know its saving rule. Such sacrifice means that God will have the first and final word about our living. He can direct us in that to which we can give ourselves; he can also direct us in what we give to ourselves. All thought and every physical thrust will thus

100

THE CHRISTIAN USE OF LIFE

serve our true religious end. The proof of any true religious concern is that the man remains under divine management; he stays altogether on God's side.

When Michael Faraday was a boy of thirteen he was engaged by a bookseller's shop as a newsboy. While delivering papers one day, he waited for someone to answer his knock. A question plagued him as he stood at the railings of the gate: "If my head were on one side of the railings and my body on the other, which side of the railings should I be on?" (The emphasis was upon the *I*.) Young Faraday proceeded to experiment; but the door was suddenly opened and the apprenhensive young philosopher drew his head back in haste. He got out with only a bumped head. His question remained unsolved, but he did learn this: it is better to be on one side of the gate or the other. That was Paul's point in calling for a self-surrender to God. The whole self must be placed on God's side, given altogether to doing his will. To act otherwise is to play with life.

6. Self-sacrifice to God is reasonable, also, because it helps to solve the problems encountered when persons meet. Paul did not stop short with the self alone before God. He had more in mind to point out than the vertical relationship of spiritual experience. He added a word at Romans 12:3 about the horizontal aspect of Christian living. He mentions the link between the self and the group. "For by the grace given to me I bid every one among you not to think of himself more highly than he ought to think, but to think with sober judgment, each according to the measure of faith which God has assigned him." It is important that we know how to see and share with each other as men under God.

101

It is no small matter when persons meet. Attitudes are expressed. There are recognized illusions of difference. Sometimes prejudice misinforms, permitting a climate of unbalance and possible tension. No properly informed Christian whose life touches another person can afford to act irresponsibly and separate. No real Christian can afford to see other men act irresponsibly and separate from each other without seeking to make peace between them.

Who but the Christian is really able to make peace? The Christian is God's agent as a peacemaker, which sometimes means that in some settings he is a pacemaker. He must be willing to stand out front, even to be hurt, in doing so. His sacrifice of self guarantees him freedom to continue his work, for it has already allowed God to work within his own life to effect the needed changes. This can mean fruitful meeting between persons, a meeting that permits no separating walls.

The master poet, Robert Frost, expressed this idea in a poem he called "Mending Walls." In five short lines he asked what building any wall would do. Who would it shut out? Who would it shut in? He would want to know this before starting to build. He concluded the poem by stating that something within man rejects walls. Something demands their destruction.

The love and will of God are against walls between man and God. They are against walls that separate man and man, brother and brother. The Christian has a ministry, in the will of God, to remove barriers from between men, to help them "meet" each other.

Back in 1923, an alert German-speaking Jew named Martin Buber published a little book which became one of the most influential studies of this century. The translated title is familiar to so many: *I and Thou*. The theme of the book is a crucial one: Community. It discusses what happens when man meets man, how to move beyond viewing other persons as *things* and make a regarded relation for true community by open dialogue. Buber asserts that such a relationship is an experience of depth. It is choosing and being chosen, feeling and responding to let the other person know that feeling; it is caring without repression. It is a life-style of encounter. It is the entrance into another person's life by both invitation and desire. All of this is in view in Buber's neat and provocative statement, "All real living is meeting."

There is a radical difference between our attitude toward things and our attitude toward persons. Buber has placed us in his debt by delineating so fruitfully the character of what is truly personal. His insights stir us to take our relationships more seriously to heart. His distinction draws a line of demarcation between community and mere organization: Organization deals with the way things are connected, while community is a living relation between persons. The distinction is not academic. It is crucial. It reminds the Christian, in particular, of what should be an abiding concern in his heart—the experience of community, true togetherness, fellowship. "Meeting" is indeed a Christian concern.

True "meeting" requires a will and ability to step across supposed boundaries. It demands openness and objectivity, deliberateness, and an assumed posture for relating. It demands creative outgoing of the whole inward self toward another. The man who has yielded himself to God in sacrifice finds it easier to confront other men. He seeks to confront them, bearing in himself something of the eternal. Self-giving first to God allows him to respond with concern to other men, to be alive, accepting, adequate. Distance has no place in this encounter. No barriers are to be recognized or allowed. This is that kind of response the late Dag Hammerskjold had in mind when he warned against those "conversations which, in their poverty, cannot hide the lack of real contact. . . . We reach out towards the other. In vain—because we have never dared to give ourselves." Real living is known in giving ourselves to God and to others, as companion. The Christian is concerned to nurture such a bond. A claiming love determines his point of view and gives him the power to act in such openness.

Some years ago when Dr. Howard Thurman was dean of Howard University Rankin Chapel, a student who heard him speak on the importance of human fellowship sought him out and questioned him about the message. "Just how far would you go with this fellowship?" the student asked.

Dr. Thurman looked smilingly at the young man, paused long enough to reflect, and then, with that easy smile, replied, "I would go all the way. I would not carry any escape clause in my back pocket." That is the kind of use to which the Christian must be committed.

7. The sacrifice of self to God is reasonable, again, because God is thereby freed to guide the labors of our lives.

The Christian use of life affects far more than our character; it will involve the service areas to which we can give ourselves in the world of men and affairs. Our endowments have a proper use in holy will and in human life.

God guides men in the labors of life. He appoints some for service within the church, to bless the church for its mission in the world. He gives others an approval for creative services they choose for the blessing of human life. But whether by direct appointment of God or his declared approval of our choices, God does guide us in the labors of our hands and the uses of our lives.

It has been many years since Horace Bushnell first preached his sermon "Every Man's Life a Plan of God," but the thesis of that sermon is still as valid. God has a personal way by which he governs our lives, making our labors serve a "good, acceptable, and perfect" Christian end.

As for his testimony about this, Billy Graham has humbly said, "I do not think God has been with me because I am more yielded or consecrated than other ministers, but I think he has been with me because of his sovereign act in choosing his servants for various tasks. I must give him the credit and the glory."[1] His life is vivid illustration of how self-surrender and divine sovereignty join hands to the glory of God and the help of needy men.

Why did Jim Elliot and the other four missionaries who gave their lives to evangelize in Auca territory take that risk? Why did their wives talk so pointedly among themselves about facing the possibilities of danger, yet did not attempt to persuade their husbands not to go? Because they all knew the risks. God was leading in the midst of the known risks. Elizabeth Elliot later explained, "Each of us knew when we married our husbands that there would never be any question about who came first—God and his work held first place in each life. It was the condition of true discipleship. . . ."[2] It was a group constrained by care for his will. Each member had sacrificed himself to God. Thus they moved from sacrifice into service.

The term, mind you, is *sacrifice*: the utter and decisive yielding of the self to God. In the demands of the term and the experience, there is the secret of being used by God. God will use only what he possesses.

From Sacrifice to Service

An actress was in her hometown, passing along one of its familiar streets, when she heard some singing from a cottage across the street. Since the door was open, she stopped outside intent to listen longer. She heard the words:

"Depth of mercy! can there be
Mercy still reserved for me?"

Someone inside the house saw the woman standing there listening and invited her to enter and share the meeting. After the meeting, she sought a copy of the book with the words to the song she had heard. She received a book and afterward was converted as she pondered those words in seriousness.

But then came the question: What about my profession? The actress began to excuse herself from the rehearsals, which in turn kept her free for a time from making appearances. She told no one as yet—especially her former associates—about her decision for Christ. The theater manager called her one morning, asking that she take the choice role in a play projected for the next week. Interestingly, it was a role she played before, somewhat earlier in her life of acting. The concern for her life pressed her at the point of her employment. She sought needed guidance from God for an answer. She took courage and informed the manager that she was leaving the stage and gave her reason. He tried to ridicule her, but the words did not turn her mind. He then appealed to her on the basis of the shortness of time before the performance, pleading the financial loss he would have if things did not go well as planned. The manager promised the actress that if she would help him fulfill that one plan he would make no further requests for her services. Sentiment moved her and she agreed to help him.

On the night of the performance everyone was in place. The play called for a song as the curtain was being raised on the first scene. The actress stepped forth to sing. The orchestra gave the melodic lead, but her voice failed. Supposing that she had panicked, the orchestra leader began again; but again the actress could not release herself in song. The theme began a third time, and in the midst of a situation that seemed foreign to her new life, the actress opened her lips to sing. Her hands were clasped and her eyes suffused with tears as she began, not the theme song of the play, but the Wesley hymn that held her heart. The show did not go on. She had promised the manager. She had intended to do her part. But a deeper, more meaningful intent held her. That actress had recognized the claim of God upon her life and knew she could not act with freedom in the old ways again.

There are those whose full surrender to God will mean for them a change of job and service role. Such persons come to realize that their new life demands a new employment context. The Christian is under necessity to make his outer life conform to the inner demands of grace. He can expect the help of God as he seeks earnestly to do this.

THE SOUL UNDER SIEGE

The sacrifice of self to God must of necessity affect one in his service in life. As William James once noted, "The great use of life is to spend it for something that will outlast it." And nothing is as lasting as service that God approves or appoints. Either one is service for God.

It is not so easy to see our involvement in a technological and industrial society as a "service for God." So many, beset by the problem of the impersonal in modern systems, ask: "How does the narrow groove of a machine fit into a divine scheme? How do mechanization and automation relate to religious concerns? Can the principle of self-sacrifice work in commercial relationships? Can religion ever be primary again in such a pluralistic culture?

Whatever his questions, the Christian must be mindful that man is never released from the moral order even if he attempts to remove himself from it. There are contradictions and insecurities to be met in relating ourselves with the world of our time. But it is at the precise point of his God-informed life that the Christian is touched by the world. His new attitudes are to serve himself,—and others. His necessary choices must be from the ground of his faith as well as his opportunities. The Christian takes God with him in his pursuits because he knows him in his person. This cannot be irrelevant in such an age as this.

Cold business facts need not disrupt the man who has moved from the sacrifice of himself to God into service, however pressurized that service role might be. The Christian must also be mindful that the will of God is often discovered *within* a situation and not always before one reaches it. Self-disclosure is still one of God's ways with men, and we cannot expect God to disclose himself to our need—whatever the age and hour. As a holder of faith, the Christian must remain alert to also interpret it. This is a crying need in our day. Is it too much to believe that God, using new men, will still do a new thing in our now old and aging order?

It might well be more than a mere social circumstance that in New Testament thought few evaluations regarding work itself appear. The stress is rather upon the *spirit* brought by the Christian to his work and service role. Faithfulness, honesty, kindness, industry are encouraged. It appears that the believer was both to make a living and use his work opportunity in alliance with God. The work of the early Christians was quite related to the social order of their times. It was in the mixture this allowed that redemptive contacts were established and nurtured. Their everyday work was not their center of meaning—their experience with Christ was. This made all their contacts positive and potential. We too shall bless our times when our work is flavored by our faith, and when our services, of whatever dimension and skill, are mellowed by our sanctity.

Robert Morrison understood this, and so became the first Protestant missionary to China. While still a student at Hoxton Academy in London, Morrison decided upon missions as his lifework. He applied to serve under the London Missionary Society and was accepted. After spending more time in preparation, studying medicine and language, Morrison sought passage to India through the East India Company. He was refused passage—that ship company was hostile to the work of missionaries. And, that company having the monopoly on all British trade at the time, Morrison was compelled to go to China by way of the United States.

THE SOUL UNDER SIEGE

A ship owner in New York sneered at hearing of Morrison's intention, and chided him. "So then, Mr. Morrison, you really expect to make an impression on the idolatry of the great Chinese Empire?"

The young man's answer was wise, tempered with redemptive faith, "No, sir, but I expect God will."

That is the optimism by which the serving Christian lives.

¹From *How I Prepare My Sermons,* edited by H. C. Brown, Jr. (Broadman Press, 1959), p. 67.
²See *Through Gates of Splendor* (Harper and Brothers, 1957), p. 175.